Discovering
STATEN
ISLAND

Discovering
STATEN
ISLAND

A 350th Anniversary Commemorative History

Charleston   London

THE
History
PRESS

Published by The History Press
Charleston, SC 29403
www.historypress.net

Cover images: Courtesy of Elizabeth Bick, the New York Public Library, the Tibetan Museum
and the Staten Island Museum. Logo design by Jason Wickersty.

First published 2011

Manufactured in the United States

ISBN 978.1.60949.170.3

Library of Congress Cataloging-in-Publication Data

Discovering Staten Island : a 350th anniversary commemorative history / edited by
Kenneth M. Gold and Lori R. Weintrob.
p. cm.
Includes bibliographical references and index.
ISBN 978-1-60949-170-3
1. Staten Island (New York, N.Y.)--History. 2. New York (N.Y.)--History. 3. Staten Island
(New York, N.Y.)--Social life and customs. 4. New York (N.Y.)--Social life and customs. 5.
Staten Island (New York, N.Y.)--Social conditions. 6. New York (N.Y.)--Social conditions. I.
Gold, Kenneth M. (Kenneth Mark), 1966- II. Weintrob, Lori Robin, 1966-
F127.S7D57 2011
974.7'26--dc22
2010053702

Notice: The information in this book is true and complete to the best of our knowledge. It is
offered without guarantee on the part of the author or The History Press. The author and

Richmond County Savings Foundation
joins in celebrating our borough
and its unique and rich history.

CONTENTS

Contents

THE CITY OF NEW YORK
OFFICE OF THE MAYOR
NEW YORK, NY 10007

January 2011

Dear Friends:

It is a great pleasure to join our City's residents and visitors alike in celebrating the 350th Anniversary of Staten Island.

Throughout our history, New York has been proud to be the world's second home—a city built and sustained by people of every background and belief. When the first Dutch settlers arrived in this area and named Staten Island in honor of their parliament, they ensured that our City would be rooted in the tolerance and freedoms that we continue to enjoy today. As we mark this significant anniversary, cultural institutions throughout New York are celebrating this milestone, and I encourage everyone to take advantage of this opportunity to learn more about *Staaten Eylandt*, Richmond County, and the poets, statesmen, and men and women from every corner of the globe who have made history on Staten Island.

On behalf of the City of New York, I offer Staten Islanders all the best wishes for an enjoyable anniversary year and continued success.

Sincerely,

Michael R. Bloomberg
Mayor

CITY OF NEW YORK
PRESIDENT
OF THE
BOROUGH OF STATEN ISLAND

JAMES P. MOLINARO
PRESIDENT

BOROUGH HALL, STATEN ISLAND, N.Y. 10301

October 5, 2010

Dear Friends:

Staten Island has always been different from the rest of New York City.

Out of the five Boroughs, it has changed the least since America became a nation. Where the other Boroughs became industrialized and had rapid population growth, Staten Island enjoyed its isolation, offering country-style living, with small towns, such as Tottenville, Westerleigh, and New Dorp, existing between acres of farmland.

Immigrants from Italy and Ireland came to Staten Island for this suburban atmosphere – knowing they could farm, keep animals, harvest oysters and clams, but still be close to Manhattan.

And that's the way things stayed, until the Verrazano Bridge opened in 1964. Suddenly Staten Island became accessible and our population grew and grew. The things that had made Staten Island so attractive – open spaces, small populations – started to disappear as buildings went up and people moved in.

Soon there were new immigrants, not just from the other Boroughs, but from Russia, Sri Lanka, Haiti, Liberia, and many other nations. They came to Staten Island because, even with this sudden growth in population, we are still a bedroom community and more suburban than the rest of New York City.

Despite the changes Staten Island has experienced over the last fifty years, we are still, in many ways, a secluded Borough of small towns. Ask someone on the street where they're from, and they'll respond "Annadale", "Port Richmond", or "St. George". The people of Staten Island enjoy the smallest population and the largest percentage of open space and parkland of any Borough in New York City.

As much as Staten Island has changed, so much has stayed the same. I want to commend si350 for celebrating the Borough's history as we approach its 350th anniversary and congratulate them on their new book.

Sincerely,

James P. Molinaro

PREFACE

Thomas Matteo

Dear Friends,

This year we will be celebrating the first permanent European settlement on Staten Island, established in 1661. Although our history actually began over ten thousand years ago, when ancestors of the Lenape lived along our southern shore, it was the Dutch, French and Belgians seeking a better life for themselves and their families who began a long tradition of people from all over the world coming to our shores. Many brave and courageous men and women continued to venture to this new land, not knowing what they would encounter but determined to make a new life.

This little island in the bay of New York is a very special place. It has given birth to and attracted to its shores many famous people from all walks of life.

Staten Island has been a land of opportunity and prosperity, for literary giants like Longfellow, Thoreau, Melville and Emerson; to business titans like Cornelius Vanderbilt, Sir Edward Cunard, Charles Goodyear, John Eberhard Faber and Donald Trump; stars of stage and screen like Paul Newman, Charlie Sheen, Ricky Schroder, Alyssa Milano, Chris Noth and Robert Loggia; and singers like Vito Piccone, Johnny Maestro, Christina Aguilera, Bobby Darin, Eileen Farrell and Wu-Tang Clan.

Others came to escape political persecution. Among these were world leaders like Giuseppe Garibaldi (Italy), Don Antonio Lopez de Santa Anna (Mexico), Gustav Struve (Germany), Lajos Kossuth (Hungary) and David Kpormakpor (Liberia). All may not be household names, but all fought for freedom and liberty in their countries, only having to flee to seek asylum among the people of Staten Island, who greeted them with open arms.

Today, we stand on the shoulders of all these men and women who came before us, those pioneers who faced hardship and death yet endured. In remembering their sacrifice, we honor our past, which enables us to embrace our future. Like those who came before us, we know not what the future holds, yet we stand ready to make a better life for our families.

I encourage you to learn more about them and the other men and women who have made Staten Island a great place to live and to raise a family.

Thomas Matteo is the Staten Island Borough historian.

INTRODUCTION AND
ACKNOWLEDGEMENTS

God might have made a more beautiful place than Staten Island, but he never did.

So wrote George William Curtis, a native New Englander, when he settled on Staten Island in the 1850s shortly after a voyage to Egypt. The expression of civic pride by Curtis—the namesake of Staten Island's first high school and an active member of the Unitarian Church in New Brighton—reminds us how rooted we are to the places we inhabit. His support of the abolition of slavery and women's suffrage and engagement in business circles and civil service reform at the local, city and national levels—notably using the press to take down New York's "Boss Tweed"—reminds us of how intertwined the island was with national concerns.

Our borough and its shores are awash in history, from Lenape trails to Dutch and French farms and Revolutionary War skirmishes, from the Atlantic Terra Cotta Company, whose products adorn Manhattan skyscrapers, to legendary sports figures and quaint historic districts. Examples abound of the importance of place, and they form the core of this book, which highlights 350 Staten Island sites of historic significance related to twelve themes: transportation, education and health, business, ethnicity, food and drink, the arts, sports, environment, politics, architecture, military and religion.

Why 350? The year 2011 will mark the 350th anniversary of the first permanent European settlement of Staten Island. In 1661, Peter Stuyvesant, the director general of New Amsterdam, granted a petition authorizing land grants to Dutch, French and Belgian families. From that moment on, Staten Island was linked to people, products and ideas throughout the world, generating a dynamic community. Today, our borough is a thriving community comprised of diverse waves of immigrants, from Irish, German, Italian and Afro-Caribbean to Sri Lankan, Korean and Liberian, and part of a global economic and cultural community.

Since 2008, more than one hundred volunteers have worked to create a calendar year that captures with meaning the diverse ways our borough has evolved. A committee of scholars, museum educators and interested citizens produced this book by identifying the 350 sites, composing the entries and selecting the accompanying photographs. The following were exceptionally generous in helping to locate, obtain and process photographs: Cara Dellatte and Patricia M. Salmon at the Staten Island Museum; Carlotta DeFillo, Sarah Clark and Maxine Friedman at the Staten Island Historical Society; Steve Zaffarano at the *Staten Island Advance*; and Steve White, Johnny Chin and Walter Palmer. Charles Markis, Charles Sachs and Meg Ventrudo graciously reviewed the entire manuscript. Chairman of the si350 Board of Directors Robert Coghlan and his predecessor, John Gustafsson, offered invaluable guidance and energy. Richmond County Savings Foundation provided financial support critical for the completion of this project. We thank all the individuals, organizations and sponsors who have contributed to this effort to showcase the island and its rich economic, cultural and political legacy, both on Staten Island and to the world at large.

This guidebook encourages readers—whether tourists or residents of New York City, whether born here or off-island—to rethink and rediscover the many fascinating places on Staten Island and, in so doing, to understand better its place in the history of New York City, the region and the world. To that end, each chapter lists its entries clockwise around the island, starting from St. George.

We emphasize the unique past of each neighborhood, organization and business listed but also the astonishing ways in which they connect to major themes in American and global history and join us to each other.

Kenneth M. Gold and Lori R. Weintrob, editors

Chapter 1

TRANSPORTATION

Kenneth M. Gold

Contributors: Jeff Cavorley and Erin Urban

Transportation on Staten Island has long revolved around two core issues: access to and from the island and movement through it. Early European settlers arrived by boat at the Watering Place and South Beach. As during the Lenape era, ferry service became the dominant mode of external transportation during the colonial era. Ferries ran intermittently from ten different locales, including Billopp's Ferry at Tottenville.

Daniel Tompkins, and later Cornelius Vanderbilt, made a fortune ferrying passengers to Brooklyn and Manhattan in the early nineteenth century. In 1886, Erastus Wiman, seeking to further orient Staten Island toward Manhattan, built the ferry terminal at St. George. The City of New York took over operation of the ferries in 1905. Today, the Staten Island Ferry serves twenty million people annually and is perhaps the most famous, internationally acclaimed symbol of Staten Island.

The routes for moving through Staten Island reflected a tension between honoring the natural world and imposing human ingenuity on it. Symbolizing this conflict, the extension of Richmond Parkway through the Greenbelt was blocked during the 1960s. Early roads, such as Richmond Terrace, Clove Road, the King's Highway and Richmond Turnpike, which followed Native American footpaths, contained sudden twists and turns due to topographical barriers that were easier to circumvent than conquer. Roads and street names also have symbolic importance to honor residents or national leaders, such as the Dr. Martin Luther King Jr. Expressway. These roads carried local commuters and regional visitors by carriage and wagon, horse car, trolley and, after 1927, bus. On occasion, transport workers on these routes have gone on strike for better wages and improved working conditions.

In the twentieth century, the construction of bridges and connecting highways unified external and internal pathways. The first bridge to reach Staten Island opened in 1889 and served the Baltimore & Ohio Railroad, but in the 1920s, the Port Authority began work on a trio of motor vehicle bridges that opened in quick succession: Outerbridge Crossing (1929), Goethals Bridge (1929) and the Bayonne Bridge (1931). With the post–World War II construction of the Staten Island Expressway and the 1964 opening of the Verrazano-Narrows Bridge—until 1981 the world's largest suspension bridge—the privileging of the automobile over other forms of transportation was nearly complete. The Staten Island Rapid Transit, with its origin dating to an 1860 trip from Eltingville to Vanderbilt Landing in Clifton, remains an important exception to this pattern.

ST. GEORGE FERRY TERMINAL

1 Ferry Terminal Drive, St. George

In 1886, Erastus Wiman built a ferry terminal at St. George that soon superseded other departure points on the North Shore and became the center for boat traffic to Manhattan. In 1905, the City of New York took over the ferry service and commissioned five new boats, named for each of the city's boroughs. New boats would be added in 1913, 1921, 1937, 1951, 1965, 1982, 1986 and 2004, while others were retired. For a short time, the terminal served a ferry that traveled to Bay Ridge, Brooklyn, but such service was discontinued with the opening of the Verrazano bridge.

The Staten Island Ferry, an internationally recognized New York City icon, celebrated its 100th anniversary under municipal control in 2005. *Courtesy of Staten Island Museum.*

U.S. LIGHTHOUSE SERVICE DEPOT/ COAST GUARD STATION

1 Lighthouse Plaza, St. George

In the 1860s, the United States Lighthouse Service established a depot in Tompkinsville, building its headquarters in the Second French Empire style. The depot supplied all materials for East Coast lighthouses, stored fuel in subterranean vaults and repaired old equipment. After a 1939 merger, it became part of the U.S. Coast Guard, Third District, and began serving cutters as well. The depot closed when the coast guard moved its base to Governor's Island in 1966. The Third District still maintains other area lighthouses, including one in New York Harbor on Robbins Reef, first built in 1839 and rebuilt in 1883. The Robbins Reef Lighthouse, once home to Katherine Walker, one of the few female U.S. lightkeepers, is expected to be transferred to the Noble Maritime Museum in 2011.

NARROWS TUNNEL SHAFT

Ferry Terminal Drive (formerly South Street), St. George

Mayor John Hylan and local civic and business leaders held groundbreaking ceremonies here for the Staten Island shaft of a freight and passenger tunnel to Brooklyn on July 19, 1923. Work on the project halted in 1925 after Governor Al Smith sided with the Port of New York Authority (later Port of Authority of New York and New Jersey, hereafter Port Authority) in a dispute over the development of New York Harbor. An earlier effort by Staten Islanders to obtain a rapid transit tunnel under the Narrows met with failure when the 1913 Dual Contracts mentioned but made no provision for such a project.

VERRAZZANO'S LANDING AND THE WATERING PLACE

Bay Street Landing and Victory Boulevard, Tompkinsville

Sailing the *Dauphin* for the French, Giovanni da Verrazzano became the first European to discover Staten Island on April 17, 1524. One of the first places on Staten Island visited by Europeans and site of an early, unsuccessful Dutch settlement, the Watering Place served, in the seventeenth and eighteenth centuries, as a final supply stop for fresh water for ships leaving New Amsterdam (later New York) for Europe. Its strategic location led the British military to encamp nearby during the American Revolution.

KING'S HIGHWAY AND RICHMOND TURNPIKE

Bay Street and Victory Boulevard, Tompkinsville

The King's Highway, named to honor the British monarch, served as the first stagecoach route on Staten Island after 1703. It ran from the Watering Place to Tottenville, along today's Van Duzer Street, Richmond Road and Amboy Road. This major thoroughfare was called King's Highway until the conclusion of the American Revolution in 1783. The Richmond Turnpike, a toll road built by New York governor Daniel Tompkins to connect Tompkinsville to Travis, dates to 1817. It was renamed Victory Boulevard after World War I.

LOMBARDI AND SONS HARLEY-DAVIDSON

440–442 Bay Street, Tompkinsville

Founded in 1905 as a general store in Graniteville, the original Lombardi and Sons made its own pasta on the premises and sold bicycles, farm equipment, groceries and other items. Responding to new trends in transportation, founder Frank Lombardi, a native of Maddolene, Italy, shifted to selling Indian motorcycles, the first American brand. In the 1920s, he moved to Stapleton and began his association with the Harley-Davidson Company. Relocating to its current site in 1932, the business remains family owned and operated.

VANDERBILT LANDING

Bay Street and Staten Island Rapid Transit (SIRT) Station, Clifton

Steam ferry service from Staten Island to New York began in 1817. The *Nautilus*, captained by John De Forest, brother-in-law of Cornelius Vanderbilt, began making trips between Whitehall Street and Tompkinsville. As Vanderbilt began acquiring local ferries, the terminal at Clifton became known as Vanderbilt Landing, and he took the title of "Commodore." With his ferries and other business interests making him one of the wealthiest men in the nation, Commodore Vanderbilt built the finest mansion on Staten Island in 1839.

Robert Moses's vision for New York City culminated in the opening of the Verrazano-Narrows Bridge only days after these tollbooths were installed on November 6, 1964. *Courtesy of Staten Island Historical Society.*

VERRAZANO-NARROWS BRIDGE

Fort Wadsworth/Arrochar

Staten Island was not the "Forgotten Borough" to Robert Moses, the "master builder" of twentieth-century New York who idealized the automobile and abhorred railroads. Construction of the Verrazano-Narrows Bridge, his and Swiss designer Othmar Ammann's last major project, began in 1959. The Italian Historical Society campaigned to have it named for the Italian explorer, against the opposition of the Staten Island Chamber of Commerce. When it opened on November 21, 1964, the Verrazano Bridge was the longest suspension bridge in the world. The Staten Island Expressway—originally named the Clove Lakes Expressway and now designated the POW/MIA Memorial Highway—linked the bridge to New Jersey. Moses's efforts to build a highway through the spine of Staten Island failed due to considerable opposition from local and environmental interests.

SOUTH BEACH TROLLEY

Father Capodanno Boulevard, South Beach

Trolley service on Staten Island began in 1892 with two companies soon engaged in a "trolley war" to establish routes. A line from St. George to the developing summer resort area of South Beach was completed in 1896. By

From 1892 to 1934, trolley cars were an important form of mass transit. At the Trolley Car Barn, Jewett Avenue, Westerleigh, are motormen Joe Dooley, W. Flannery and William Lyons (seated and center, they are the first, third and fifth men). *Courtesy of Staten Island Historical Society.*

1913, several trolley lines ran across the island. Faced with the increasing unprofitability of the five-cent fare, the City of New York took over the Midland Electric Railroad Company in 1920 and replaced its lines with bus routes in 1927. Other trolley routes were taken over by the Tompkins Bus Corporation in 1931.

HYLAN BOULEVARD

Rosebank to Tottenville

Hylan Boulevard is a prominent exception to the island's pattern of major roads having colonial antecedents. Its first component, from Grasmere to Oakwood, opened as Southfield Avenue around 1900. Between 1924 and 1927, additional sections linked Rosebank to Tottenville. Mayor John Hylan was quite popular on Staten Island for his support of a Narrows tunnel and other public improvements, though the decision to rename the expanded road after a sitting mayor stirred partisan rancor. The boulevard was notable at the time for its width of one hundred feet.

ELTINGVILLE RAILROAD TRAIN STATION

Richmond Avenue and Eltingville Boulevard, Eltingville

The Staten Island Railroad opened for business in 1860, extending from Vanderbilt Landing in Clifton to Eltingville. Named after the company president and nicknamed the "huge iron monster," the locomotive Albert Journeay made three trips daily. The tracks were soon extended to Tottenville. To reach St. George, a 985-foot-long tunnel was constructed under federal land in 1886. The public celebrated the conversion of the St. George–Tottenville line from steam to electric power in 1925. In 2010, the line celebrated its 150th anniversary and today serves over four million riders annually.

Originally a steam-powered line, the Staten Island Railroad converted to electric power in 1925. The public celebration on July 1, 1925, in Eltingville is captured here. *Courtesy of Staten Island Historical Society.*

OUTERBRIDGE CROSSING

Richmond Valley

Completed in 1928, this span over the Arthur Kill to Perth Amboy was named for Staten Islander Eugenius H. Outerbridge, the first chairman of the Port Authority. The Goethals Bridge, opened on the same day in 1928 and named for the builder of the Panama Canal, traverses the Arthur Kill farther north between Howland Hook and Elizabeth. These bridges represented the first major accomplishment of the fledgling Port Authority. Before the bridge, Tottenville was connected to Perth Amboy by ferry, operated by Billopp initially and much later by the SIRT.

BONEYARD AND OLD BLAZING STAR FERRY

Arthur Kill Road, Rossville

Started in the 1930s as part of Witte's (now Donjon Marine Company) Scrapyard, the Boneyard contains a cornucopia of nautical relics. These ferryboats, tugboats, passenger steamers, navy vessels and fireboats were built over the past century. Notable hulls include the *Abram S. Hewitt* and SS *New Bedford*. At this site, Anthony Wright operated the *Old Blazing Star Ferry* to Woodbridge from 1722 to 1773.

RICHMOND CREEK AND FRESH KILLS BRIDGES

Arthur Kill and Richmond Roads, Richmond;
Richmond Avenue, Greenridge

In 1845, a still-standing arched fieldstone structure replaced a wooden bridge over Richmond Creek long used by travelers. Demanding a more direct route from Greenridge to Port Richmond, a citizens committee— incorporated as the Port Richmond and Fresh Kills Plank Road Company—opened the Fresh Kills toll bridge (also called the Richmond Avenue Bridge) in 1853. The toll was two cents for foot passengers, four cents for horseback travelers and single horse vehicles, six cents for multiple-horse vehicles and one penny apiece for heads of cattle, sheep and swine. Declared unsafe in 1880, it was replaced with a new publicly built iron bridge in 1896 and a concrete bridge in 1931.

STATEN ISLAND LIGHTHOUSE

Originally known as Richmond Light, the Staten Island Lighthouse, Lighthouse Hill, has been in continuous use since 1912. *Courtesy of Staten Island Historical Society.*

Edinboro Road, Lighthouse Hill

Commonly referred to as "Richmond Light," the Staten Island Lighthouse was built on Richmond Hill (now Lighthouse Hill) in 1912. Resting on a limestone base 141 feet above sea level, the stately octagonal lighthouse serves ships navigating the Ambrose Channel in Lower New York Bay. The 90-foot lighthouse became a New York City landmark in 1968. Local citizens, following the path of former volunteer caretaker Joe Esposito, help preserve this working treasure. Other early lighthouses on Staten Island were located at Fort Wadsworth, New Dorp, Prince's Bay and Shooter's Island.

HISTORIC RICHMOND TOWN'S CARRIAGE FACTORY

Richmond Road between Court and St. Patrick's Places, Richmond (Former Site)

One of the earliest carriage factories on Staten Island, Isaac Marsh's business opened in the 1840s on Richmond Hill Road. In 1854, it moved to a new three-story brick building, featuring a blacksmith and wood shop, a painting workshop and a showroom. The factory prospered during the Civil War years, and a second building was constructed in 1869. Upon Marsh's death in 1896, John Schweibert took over operations, purchased the factory in 1901 and oversaw a transition from carriage manufacture to automobile repair. The factory closed in 1940.

STATEN ISLAND AIRPORT

Richmond Avenue at Richmond Hill Road,
New Springville (Former Site)

McCormick's Staten Island Airport was located at what later became the site of Pergament Center, west of the Staten Island Mall. Note the drive-in theater in the distance. *Courtesy of Staten Island Historical Society.*

Air travel arrived on Staten Island in the twentieth century, and by 1947, four airports operated on the island. In 1941, Ed McCormick, a local businessman and pilot, opened and ran the Staten Island Airport. At more than 350 acres, the field offered pilots two runways (though one saw little use after it was shortened by the placement of a drive-in movie theater) and promoted its location as a mere forty minutes from Times Square. After its closure in 1965, the site became the Staten Island Mall. The three additional airfields were the Richmond County Airport, Donovan Hughes Airport and Miller Field.

HOWLAND HOOK/GULFPORT
SEE BUSINESS AND THE ECONOMY

SHOOTER'S ISLAND

Kill van Kull, Mariners Harbor

Shooter's Island earned its name from the geese hunting done by Dutch colonists, but it became most noted for its shipyard. First housing a shipyard in the 1860s, in 1900, the Townsend Downey Shipyard started producing some of the finest yachts in the world. These included the *Meteor* for Kaiser Wilhelm II of Germany and the *Atlantic*, which set a world record that still stands for the fastest ship crossing of the Atlantic. The Standard Shipbuilding Company put out a ship a month for the navy after America's entry into World War I.

BAYONNE BRIDGE

Martin Luther King Jr. Expressway, Elm Park

The longest steel-arch bridge in the world when it opened in 1931, the Bayonne Bridge was the third span to New Jersey—and first over the Kill van Kull—constructed by the Port Authority. Designed by renowned bridge builder Othmar Ammann and architect Cass Gilbert, its construction, without blocking sea traffic below, posed a technical challenge met by prefabricating forty truss segments elsewhere, transporting them to the site and lifting them into place. The bridge was designed to accommodate two rail lines, and its pedestrian walkway provides the only access to Staten Island by foot or bicycle.

NORTH SHORE RAIL LINE STATION

Park Avenue and Church Street, Port Richmond

In the late nineteenth century, Erastus Wiman entered into a partnership with the B&O Railroad that would result in the extension of rail lines west of Clifton. In 1884, the first train pulled into the Tompkinsville station; two years later, service to Elm Park opened; and in 1889, a railroad bridge was constructed over the Arthur Kill. Electrification of the line was completed in 1925, but ridership declined after the city takeover of the buses in 1948. By the 1950s, service was reduced to single-car trains, and the last trip was made in 1953. The Port Richmond station survives as a visible reminder of this line, and studies have been conducted to reopen it, most recently in 2002.

DECKER'S FERRY AND INN

Ferry Street, Port Richmond (Former Site)

The origins of a ferry line between Port Richmond and Bergen Point date back to the early eighteenth century, when Jacob Corsen opened a ferry. In 1774, Isaac Decker began operating the ferry and an inn with the "best liquors, eatables and lodgins." During the Revolutionary War, Decker's ferry was one of only two ferry lines officially recognized by the British military,

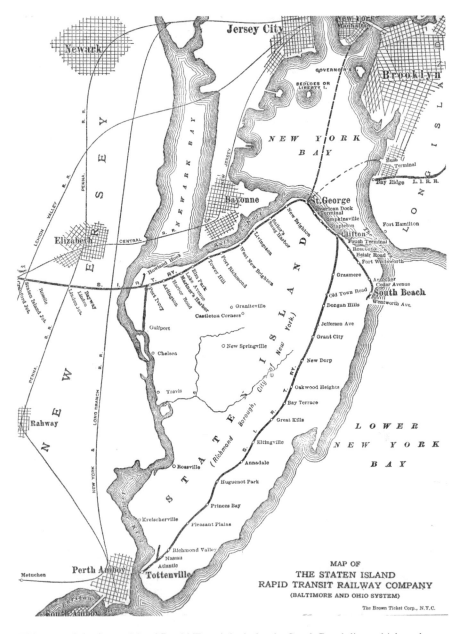

This map of the Staten Island Rapid Transit includes the South Beach line, which took tourists to their favorite resort destinations. *Courtesy of Staten Island Historical Society.*

"THE FUTURE OF TRANSPORTATION AND MOBILITY ON STATEN ISLAND"

Jonathan Peters, PhD, Professor of Finance, College of Staten Island

As Staten Island moves into the latter part of its fourth century, its communities face unique challenges to solve its transportation needs. Staten Island had the highest population growth of any county in New York state; from 1990 to 2000, there was a 17.1 percent increase, with another 40 percent increase expected by 2030. It now faces a rising population density despite the continued absence of dense centers of housing found in the other boroughs. As the only borough of New York City that was never served by the NYC Subway, Staten Island faces unique transportation challenges.

Having more registered vehicles than Manhattan with one-third of the population, Staten Island's heavy dependence on private automobile travel has resulted in recurring and persistent traffic congestion. The weak mass transportation system leaves residents with the longest average commute in the United States (43.1 minutes each way) and the longest average mass transit commute in New York City (68.4 minutes each way). Moving forward, Staten Islanders must stabilize the growth in private automobile travel and convert more of their local and commuting trips to mass transit.

Modern transit options on Staten Island can be created by deploying new light rail lines or bus rapid transit systems on existing roads with wide easements and on abandoned or little-used freight rail corridors. Three routes have considerable promise: the North Shore Rail line, stretching from St. George to Mariners Harbor; the West Shore corridor, utilizing the freight line to Travis and then the West Shore Expressway median for transit services; and a route down the center of Staten Island that primarily runs along the Dr. Martin Luther King Jr. Expressway and Richmond Avenue.

Finally, there exists the potential to extend the Hudson Bergen Light Rail Line from Bayonne, New Jersey, to Staten Island over the existing Bayonne Bridge. This bridge, the only Staten Island bridge with rail easements, has the potential to extend modern mass transit services to the North and West Shores of Staten Island, allowing low-income residents to access jobs in Jersey City and Manhattan and reducing commuting times significantly.

while Patriot soldiers used it to cross to Staten Island and assault the British. In 1889, the landing was moved from Ferry Street to the foot of Richmond Avenue, and service continued until 1961.

MEMOLY MOTORS

Richmond Terrace near Jewett Avenue, West Brighton (Former Site)

Staten Islanders embraced the automobile. By 1945, the island contained thirty automobile dealerships, employing 255 people and recording nearly $6 million in sales. Several lined Castleton Avenue in West Brighton, while some of the oldest and most well-known dealers were found in Port Richmond. These included the Cornell Motor Car Company, established in 1909 and selling Cadillacs, and Memoly Motors, which sold Dodges and Plymouths.

CADDELL'S DRY DOCK

Richmond Terrace and Broadway, West New Brighton

Caddell's Dry Dock is the oldest operating shipyard in New York Harbor. Started in Brooklyn in 1903 by John Caddell and two partners, the yard found a new home on Staten Island in 1915. Since then the shipyard has maintained thousands of ships. Some of its work can be seen aboard South Street Seaport vessels *Wavertree*, *Peking* and *Ambrose*, as well as on the *Halfe Moon* (the replica of Henry Hudson's ship). On the more modern side, Caddell's Dry Dock Co. has maintained everything from tugboats and barges to naval vessels.

NATIVE AMERICAN FOOTPATH

Richmond Terrace at Alaska Street, West New Brighton

Richmond Terrace, laid out around 1705, shares similar origins to most other early roads on Staten Island. With several Lenape villages on Staten Island located along the North Shore, a Native American footpath developed to connect them. This path became the first road built by European settlers to connect Port Richmond to a ferry at what would later become St. George.

BENNETT'S BICYCLES

517 Jewett Avenue, Port Richmond

In 1896, Nicholas Bennett opened a hardware and general store—featuring the first telegraph key on Staten Island—near Fort Wadsworth. His son, Nick, became a plumber but focused his energies on selling bicycles in the store, now in Stapleton, after losing his plumbing trucks during the Great Depression. Forced to relocate to make room for the construction of the Stapleton Houses, Bennett's moved to its current location in 1957. Nicholas eventually passed the business to his son, George, whose sons George and Tom Bennett are now the fourth generation to run what they proclaim is the oldest bike store in New York City.

STAGECOACH ROUTE

Manor Road and Victory Boulevard, Castleton Corners

With Bodine's Inn at the service of travelers, Castleton Corners was a stop on the stagecoach route to Philadelphia, as well as the terminus of routes to West New Brighton and Vanderbilt Landing. A horse car route ran along Manor Road through Castleton Corners in the late 1900s. In the twentieth century, it has functioned as a vital local bus and automobile route.

CLOVE ROAD

Sunnyside

Its name derived from the Dutch word for cleft, Clove Road was built on a pathway between Emerson and Grymes Hills. It became one of the most important routes for moving by foot, horse car, trolley, automobile or bus from the North Shore to the center of Staten Island.

WITTEMANN AIRPLANE MANUFACTURING

Little Clove Road at Ocean Terrace, Sunnyside

Charles Wittemann established arguably the world's first airplane factory. In 1898, Wittemann experimented with a kite large enough to lift him off the ground and subsequently constructed his first successful glider. He began producing gliders commercially in 1905, designed and built his first airplane in 1906 and filled orders for gliders and planes, including Thomas Baldwin's Red Devil. After building two hundred gliders and thirty-five airplanes, the Staten Island plant was shut down in 1914, and the growing company moved to the site of modern-day Newark Airport.

Chapter 2

EDUCATION AND HEALTH

Patricia Tooker and Andrew Wilson

Contributors: Diane Arneth, Kristin Finn, Peter Levine, Michael Marando and Arleen Ryback

Two keys to Staten Island's quality of life are its education and healthcare. The island's schools range from the oldest surviving schoolroom in America, Voorlezer's House (circa 1695), to three modern universities and more than one hundred public, private and parochial schools. Its healthcare institutions also began remarkably early, notably with the nationally significant Quarantine Station and Hospital (1799–1858), precursor to Ellis Island.

Henry David Thoreau tutored the nephew of Ralph Waldo Emerson on Emerson Hill. Anna Leonowens, the real-life tutor of the king of Siam's children in *The King and I*, ran a West New Brighton school. Tottenville High School science teacher Paul Zindel and McKee Vocational School teacher Frank McCourt both won the Pulitzer Prize.

In 1812, New York state, under the leadership of Governor Daniel Tompkins, authorized the establishment of local school districts. Staten Islanders subsequently attended schools known by their district name and number, such as Westfield Township District School No. 5. Following consolidation with New York in 1898, the former district schools were renumbered and referred to primarily by their new designations, like P.S. 1 in Tottenville or P.S. 20 in Port Richmond. Some public and parochial schools are also named for civic activists, such as George W. Curtis, Berta Dreyfus or Monsignor Joseph A. Farrell. The island is dotted with art schools, dance schools, language schools, music schools, religious schools, home-based tutors—the variety is endless. The Dutch Voorlezer would be proud.

Sites associated with healthcare on Staten Island are no less impressive. The National Institute of Health in Washington, D.C., traces its origins to the 1887 laboratory of public health at the Marine Hospital in Stapleton. That same year, the Russell Smith Infirmary moved from its founder's private home (a common site for nineteenth-century hospitals) to the now-beloved "Castle," its "cornerless" rooms thought to reduce the collection of germs. In the twentieth century, Seaview Hospital was the largest tuberculosis facility in the nation. Even the tragic case of Willowbrook provided a legal precedent for improving the conditions of mentally ill around the world. A review of evidence-based practices can help borough agencies move forward creatively to serve the needs of diverse communities.

CURTIS HIGH SCHOOL

105 Hamilton Avenue, St. George

Curtis High School, named for civic leader George William Curtis, was the first public building constructed after the 1898 consolidation of New York City. *Courtesy of Staten Island Museum.*

A monument to a new era, Curtis High School opened in 1904 as the first public building constructed on Staten Island after the consolidation of the five boroughs and its first high school. Its collegiate gothic architecture points backward to the Western academic tradition, and its namesake was George William Curtis, a nationally acclaimed writer and supporter of abolition and women's suffrage. Growing from 750 to more than 2,500 students, Curtis is the home of many outstanding academic and extracurricular programs and maintains an active alumni association. Curtis is the alma mater of many of Staten Island's most accomplished athletes. These include Bobby Thomson, who hit the most celebrated home run in baseball history; Abe Kiviat, a multiple world record holder in the mile and silver medalist in the 1912 Olympic Games; National Basketball Hall of Famer Elmer Ripley; and legendary high school football coaches Sal Somma and Andy Barberi.

Staten Island Museum and Archives

75 Stuyvesant Place, St. George
New Snug Harbor Location: 1000 Richmond Terrace,
Buildings A, B and H, New Brighton

Founded in 1881 as the Natural Science Association of Staten Island, the Staten Island Museum (SIM) was established by fourteen collectors of natural science specimens concerned that the "rapid growth of the community obliterated many of our most interesting natural objects." SIM became public in 1908 and was soon a lively center for culture, research and education. Dedicated to interdisciplinary programs and collections in science, art and history, SIM remains New York City's only general interest museum.

Quarantine Station

Hyatt Street, Tompkinsville

In 1799, nearly a century before the opening of Ellis Island, Staten Island was designated as a quarantine station to protect the health of residents of the port of New York against contagious diseases. The detention hospital stood in Tompkinsville, on William B. Townsend's land. Dr. Richard Bayley, first health officer of the port of New York, served at the quarantine station until his death in 1811. Local residents, fearful of contagion and interested in promoting higher real estate prices, burned the facility in 1858. Other quarantine stations were in Prince's Bay, Rosebank and Hoffman and Swinburne Islands, where immigrants with contagious diseases were housed until 1937.

Alice Austen, one of America's first celebrated female photographers, captured the processing of immigrants at the Hoffman Island Quarantine on May 23, 1901. *Courtesy of Staten Island Historical Society.*

COMMUNITY HEALTH ACTION OF STATEN ISLAND (CHASI)

56 Bay Street, St. George

Founded in 1988 by HIV-infected community members, advocates and service providers, the Staten Island AIDS Task Force (now CHASI) is the only boroughwide AIDS service organization. It works to prevent the spread of HIV and serve the needs of those with HIV/AIDS and their families. CHASI has also developed educational and social programs for the borough's lesbian, gay, bisexual and transgender (LGBT) communities.

U.S. MARINE HOSPITAL/BAYLEY-SETON HOSPITAL

75 Vanderbilt Avenue, Clifton

On October 1, 1831, Staten Island's first hospital, the Seaman's retreat, opened for retired naval and commercial sailors. After that institution moved to Sailors' Snug Harbor, New Brighton, in 1883, Marine Health Service (MHS) officer Dr. Joseph J. Kinyoun established in 1887 a bacteriological laboratory, from which the National Institute of Health evolved. The MHS, renamed the Public Health Service in 1951, took on the responsibility for several public health issues. The Sisters of Charity purchased this twenty-acre property in 1980, renaming it for Dr. Richard Bayley (quarantine doctor) and his daughter, Elizabeth Ann (Mother Seton), founder of the Sisters of St. Vincent de Paul order (see page 45).

STATEN ISLAND UNIVERSITY HOSPITAL

475 Seaview Avenue (North Site), South Beach
375 Seguine Avenue (South Site, Former Richmond Memorial
Hospital), Prince's Bay

Staten Island University Hospital's history is the story of two hospitals and three centuries of medical advances. In 1861, a small infirmary opened on Staten Island's North Shore to treat the poor, who lacked access to

Staten Island University Hospital celebrates its 150th anniversary in 2011. From a one-room clinic, it moved to the six-acre "Castle" site, shown here, from 1890 to 1979. It is currently housed in two state-of-the-art facilities. *Courtesy of Staten Island University Hospital.*

medical care. An initiative of the Richmond County Medical Society, the infirmary relied on a women's auxiliary—now the nation's oldest continuous auxiliary—to appeal to the community for funds. By 1900, the infirmary had served one thousand patients, including veterans of the Spanish-American War, with inoculations and newly developed X-rays. Renamed the Staten Island Hospital in 1917, the facility by then cared for all borough residents and went on to sponsor noted research on poliomyelitis serum and host the Wagner College School of Nursing. In need of space, Staten Island Hospital moved in 1979 from its "Castle Building" on Castleton Avenue to its seventeen-acre Seaview Avenue home.

Berta and Louis Dreyfus became benefactors of Richmond Memorial Hospital, which opened in 1919 in two wooden farmhouses on Seguine Avenue and dedicated itself to "local sons" who died in World War I. By 1929, Richmond Memorial's two-floor, brick hospital building accommodated obstetrical patients and expanded capabilities for medical and surgical patients. The two hospitals merged in 1987, and today, SIUH has 715 beds.

"LETTER FROM A GRANDSON: STATEN ISLAND UNIVERSITY HOSPITAL AT ITS 150ᵀᴴ ANNIVERSARY"

Anthony C. Ferreri, President and Chief Executive Officer of Staten Island University Hospital

About three years ago, a nurse manager came into the administrative offices of Staten Island University Hospital carrying a very old and large book with pages that were clearly brittle and faded. The book was a register identifying all patient admissions for 1928–1929. This manager found the book while cleaning the top of a file cabinet in the seven-year-old "Heart Tower."

The register provided a comprehensive look at what the hospital offered some eighty years earlier. Details on each patient were meticulously and identically handwritten in several columns across two pages. Columns included information on the referring physician, payee, diagnosis, "nativity" (i.e. place of birth), citizenship, address and outcome.

A lifelong Staten Islander, I became curious and decided to browse the pages, looking for surnames that would be familiar. To my amazement, I came across the name "Anthony DiSerafino," a patient who had been admitted on May 17, 1929, with an injured and infected hand. He was referred by the clinic and was discharged after six days. His bill was paid by "NYC," probably because he could not afford to pay for his care.

After all, this was years before Medicaid, workers' compensation and Blue Cross and Blue Shield. His occupation was listed as "Laborer," and he lived on Nugent Street in Egbertville. He was twenty-nine years old at the time, and the outcome listed his condition at discharge as "Relieved."

I asked my mother if she remembered her father's hospitalization so many years ago. She was six years old at the time, and to this day, she thought that his only hospitalization during his sixty-nine years was at the time of his death in 1963. She then asked her older brother, Patsy. He clearly remembered the hospitalization: "Papa was hurt at work and was hospitalized to treat the resulting infection."

I knew that if I searched the pages for a connection, I'd find one. I consider myself blessed that I found this "message" from the past. It's a message that further supports my personal conviction that access to healthcare is everyone's right and further demonstrates the hospital's mission to provide quality care to all, regardless of ability to pay.

Staten Island Hospital has lived up to that mission for 150 years. Just as hospital staff treated and "relieved" my grandfather, they recently delivered my grandson. As it was in 1861, in 1929 and in 2011, the hospital is here for all who come through its doors for care.

Staten Island Academy

715 Todt Hill Road, Todt Hill

The Staten Island Academy is the oldest private school on Staten Island, serving four hundred students in grades pre-K through twelve. Organized by a group of educators in a union with the Methfessel Institute of Stapleton, the Staten Island Academy and Latin School opened on September 5, 1884. In the 1890s, the school relocated to the corner of Wall Street and Academy Place in St. George. In the 1940s, the lower and middle schools of the academy moved to Dongan Hall, formerly the estate of Franklin Delano Roosevelt's secretary of state, Edward Stettinius. In 1964, ground was broken on the Todt Hill campus to build facilities to house the entire school. Dongan Hall was destroyed by fire in 1975.

Eger Lutheran Nursing Home

120 Meisner Avenue, Egbertville

Chester Aldrich (1871–1940), architect of the Staten Island Savings Bank, and his sister, Amey, operated a convalescent home for boys ages twelve to twenty at this site. In 1924, Carl Michael Eger of Oslo, Norway, purchased the serenely wooded twenty-two-acre campus to build an institution for elderly Norwegian men and women. Today, Eger Health Care and Rehabilitative Center offers 378 nursing beds.

Historic Richmond Town's Voorlezer's House

Arthur Kill Road, Richmond

The Voorlezer's House, one of the most important surviving examples of seventeenth-century Dutch settlements in New York, is the oldest school building still standing in America. Built circa 1695, it served as home, school and church for the Dutch Reformed congregation's voorlezer, an assistant pastor. The voorlezer (translated from the Dutch "lay reader") was a layman whose primary job was keeping church records and leading services in the absence of the pastor. He also taught children reading, writing, arithmetic and religious catechism. It served as a private residence and store to French, Irish and Jewish families until 1936. After restoration, it became a National Historic Landmark in 1961.

MONSIGNOR FARRELL HIGH SCHOOL

2900 Amboy Road, Oakwood Heights

In April 2011, Monsignor Farrell High School will be celebrating its fiftieth anniversary. This diocesan high school was established as part of a citywide campaign by Cardinal Francis Spellman, archbishop of New York. Among the accomplishments of Monsignor Joseph A. Farrell—its namesake—were his role in founding St. Peter's Boys High School in 1917 and Manhattan Junior College (1935–1943), during his tenure as pastor, vicar and civic leader on Staten Island from 1900 to 1960. The school's Irish club honors his place in New York City's Irish history. Parochial education on Staten Island dates back as early as 1853, with the establishment of the school affiliated with St. Mary's Church on Bay Street, Rosebank.

MOUNT LORETTO

6581 Hylan Boulevard, Pleasant Plains

SEE ALSO ENVIRONMENT, RELIGION AND SPORTS

The Mission for the Immaculate Virgin for the Protection of Homeless and Destitute Children began in 1882 when Father John C. Drumgoole brought homeless newsboys sheltered at the Mission on Lafayette Street, Manhattan, to this farm. Fort Smith was originally a redoubt in the American Revolution. More than 900 boys and girls (and, in the Great Depression, about 1,500) from the ages of six to eighteen attended trade school and farmed at Mount Loretto. In 1951, it still had one hundred cows providing milk (pasteurized on site) to the orphans. At the same time, it boasted an outstanding sports program. More recently, the campus has housed Project Hospitality, Saint Francis Food Pantry, the CYO-MIV Community Center, the Staten Island Sports Hall of Fame and Museum, IS/PS 25 and a nature preserve.

P.S. 1 Annex

58 Summit Street, Annex at the Corner of Yetman and Academy Avenues, Tottenville

Currently the oldest public school in use on Staten Island, the P.S. 1 Annex was erected in 1878 as Westfield Township District School No. 5. The school expanded in 1896 to include two upper grades, initially one of the three high school departments established on Staten Island. Westfield District School No. 5 became P.S. No. 1, Borough of Richmond, after the consolidation of Greater New York in 1898. The current P.S. 1 building, 58 Summit Street, was built in 1905.

Tottenville Branch of the New York Public Library

7430 Amboy Road, Tottenville

Tottenville boasted the first public library on Staten Island. In 1899, the Philemon Club of Tottenville, a local women's organization, and the men's Philo Debating Society established the Tottenville Library Association and Free Library in two rooms of a Johnson Avenue house. Philanthropist Andrew Carnegie offered to build a library for all communities that would agree to stock and staff them. The Tottenville library merged with the New York Public Library (NYPL) following consolidation. On November 26, 1904, the Tottenville branch moved into its present building, designed by Staten Island architect John Carrère and his partner, Thomas Hastings, who also designed Borough Hall and the Fifth Avenue home of the NYPL.

The Staten Island Book Wagon stopped in Eltingville in the early 1900s. *Courtesy of New York Public Library.*

39

STATEN ISLAND CHINESE SCHOOL

33 Ferndale Avenue, New Springville

Staten Island has a long tradition of schools and organizations that strive to maintain the languages and cultures of the home countries of its immigrant populations. The first one serving its Chinese population was the Staten Island Chinese School, now celebrating its fortieth anniversary. Started in a local church with seven students, the Chinese School now enrolls more than one hundred children studying Mandarin or Cantonese.

SEA VIEW HOSPITAL/FARM COLONY

460 Brielle Avenue, Manor Heights

Sea View Hospital was the largest tubercular hospital in the world when it opened in 1914, and it then grew from a nine-hundred- to a two-thousand-bed capacity. Operated first by the Department of Hospitals of the City of New York until 1961 and then by the Department of Public Welfare, Sea View Hospital today serves as a three-hundred-bed, long-term care facility. It is best known as a long-term care traumatic brain injury unit, the first of its kind in New York state. The Richmond County Poor House opened in 1829, and in 1903 it became the NYC Farm Colony, where residents farmed their own food.

Sea View Hospital was the largest tubercular hospital in the world when it opened in 1914. In the 1950s, its doctors pioneered the cure for the disease. *Courtesy of Staten Island Historical Society.*

RICHMOND COUNTY MEDICAL SOCIETY

460 Brielle Avenue, Manor Heights

To serve dependents of Civil War soldiers, the Richmond County Medical Society (RCMS) and Dr. William C. Anderson helped found the Samuel R. Smith Infirmary. It was the first voluntary hospital on Staten Island. RCMS physicians have served in hospitals and medical centers throughout the city.

NURSERY AND CHILDREN'S HOSPITAL

Near Melba Street and Holden Boulevard, Willowbrook

Originally founded by Staten Islander Mary A. DuBois in 1854, this facility represented a merger of an 1823 hospital and the New York infant asylum. With 2,155 women and children patients in 1899, this "country branch" of the New York Nursery and Children's Hospital promoted recognition of women physicians including Anna Lukens. As medical treatment began to replace institutional admissions, the hospital closed by 1905.

COLLEGE OF STATEN ISLAND (CSI), CITY UNIVERSITY OF NEW YORK (CUNY)

2800 Victory Boulevard, Willowbrook

CUNY traces its beginning to an 1847 public referendum that provided tuition-free higher education for residents of New York City, and it still offers affordable, quality education to New York City. CSI was founded in 1976 through the union of Staten Island Community College (SICC) and Richmond College. SICC opened in 1955 on the Sunnyside campus that today houses the Petrides School. Richmond College, founded in 1965, offered undergraduate and graduate degrees to students in their third and fourth years. In 1993, the College of Staten Island moved to the renovated grounds of the former Halloran Hospital and Willowbrook State School. Today it serves approximately fourteen thousand undergraduate and graduate students on the largest college campus in CUNY.

HALLORAN HOSPITAL
SEE MILITARY HISTORY

WILLOWBROOK STATE SCHOOL

2800 Victory Boulevard, Willowbrook

Willowbrook State School served children with developmental disabilities from 1947 to 1987. Designed to accommodate four thousand residents, the school had a population of six thousand by 1965 and was the biggest state-run institution for the mentally handicapped in the United States. Overcrowded conditions as well as questionable medical practices and abuse were brought to light in 1971–1972 by the *Staten Island Advance* and Geraldo Rivera (WABC-TV). Public outcry led to its eventual closure in 1987, and resulting civil rights laws protecting the disabled have made a global impact. Parts of the site were incorporated into a new campus for the College of Staten Island in 1993.

INSTITUTE FOR BASIC RESEARCH IN DEVELOPMENTAL DISABILITIES (IBR)

1050 Forest Hill Road, Willowbrook

Opened in 1968, the IBR is a facility of the New York State Office of Mental Retardation and Developmental Disabilities. The IBR conducts research, both basic and clinical, on developmental disabilities. Service programs include the George A. Jervis Clinic, named for the first director of the IBR. Among the institute's educational activities is a graduate studies program, the Center for Developmental Neuroscience and Developmental Disabilities, in collaboration with the College of Staten Island.

P.S. 20 (FORMER BUILDING)

160 Heberton Avenue, Port Richmond

The site of a school since 1842, the original P.S. 20 was a two-story brick building and stable serving as classrooms. The Romanesque Revival

Civic pride is projected by the lofty bell tower and clock of Port Richmond's P.S. 20, site of the borough's first high school classes. *Photograph by F. Simonson. Courtesy of Staten Island Historical Society.*

building that now stands on the site was constructed from 1891 to 1898 and was designated a New York City landmark in 1988. It now serves as Parkside Senior Housing after revitalization by the Northfield Community Local Development Corporation. In Veterans Park, the Putnam Memorial—a large decorative drinking fountain—honors Eugene G. Putnam (1865–1913), principal of P.S. 20 for seventeen years. Renamed for former District 31 superintendent Christy Cugini, P.S. 20 relocated to 161 Park Avenue.

Staten Island YMCA

651 Broadway, West New Brighton; 3911 Richmond Avenue, Eltingville; and 3939 Richmond Avenue, Eltingville

Founded in 1852 and opening a Stapleton office in 1857, the YMCA of Greater New York is the largest youth-serving organization in New York City. The Staten Island YMCA dedicated its headquarters on Broadway in 1953, organized the South Shore branch as its extension in 1977 and opened a full-service facility in Eltingville in 1997. The YMCA Counseling Service opened substance abuse prevention and treatment programs on the South Shore in 1980 and later brought these services and the New Americans Welcome Center to Clifton.

Staten Island Zoo

614 Broadway, West New Brighton

In 1933, the Staten Island Zoological Society formed to create and administer a zoo to be located in Clarence T. Barrett Park. Construction began as part of the federal government's works program, and three years later, the Staten Island Zoo was born. The zoo's long-standing mission is to instill in children an appreciation of living creatures. Historically known for its reptile (particularly snakes) and amphibian collections, the zoo was also the first in America to employ a full-time female veterinarian, hiring Dr. Patricia O'Connor in 1942. Tropical forests and African savannah exhibits were installed in the 1990s.

WAGNER COLLEGE

631 Howard Avenue, Grymes Hill

Wagner College was founded in Rochester in 1883 as a German-language preparatory school for the Lutheran seminary. After a donation from John G. Wagner, the institution was renamed in memory of his son, George. Frederic Sutter, an early graduate who had established a ministry at Staten Island's Trinity Evangelical Lutheran Church, facilitated the school's 1918 move to the former estate of shipping magnate Edward Cunard on Grymes Hill. There, Wagner transformed into an American-style liberal arts college, constructed its trademark Main Hall in 1930 and began admitting women in 1933. Today, recognized as a Top 25 regional college, it serves more than two thousand students.

ST. JOHN'S UNIVERSITY

300 Howard Avenue, Grymes Hill

St. John's University was founded in 1870 in the Bedford-Stuyvesant neighborhood of Brooklyn by the Roman Catholic Vincentian Fathers. The Staten Island campus—once the estate of John H. Gans, president of the Gans Steamship Line and a German immigrant—became the site of Notre Dame College. Founded by Sister Helen Flynn, who ran an extension of Fordham University on the campus of nearby Notre Dame Academy, Notre Dame served as a women's college for over thirty years. In 1971, Notre Dame became part of St. John's University in Brooklyn, offering undergraduate degrees in liberal arts, business and education. Today, the Staten Island campus has expanded to sixteen acres and serves more than two thousand students.

RICHMOND UNIVERSITY MEDICAL CENTER

355 Bard Avenue, New Brighton
75 Vanderbilt Avenue, Clifton

Richmond University Medical Center, a 510-bed facility with 2,300 employees delivering 3,000 babies and serving 25,000 in- and outpatients annually, originated as St. Vincent's Hospital. Established by the Sisters of Charity of New York, St. Vincent's opened in 1903 as a 74-bed facility on the site of the former W.T. Garner mansion. Sisters of Charity Healthcare System subsequently acquired the former U.S. Public Health Service Hospital in Clifton, renaming it Bayley-Seton Hospital (see page 34). In 2006, St. Vincent's was sold to Bayonne Medical Center and spun off as Richmond University Medical Center (RUMC).

DR. SAMUEL MACKENZIE ELLIOTT HOUSE

69 Delafield Place, Randall Manor

Scottish-born Samuel MacKenzie Elliott achieved fame as one of America's earliest oculists and eye surgeons. Elliott's New York practice boasted patients like John Jacob Astor, Peter Cooper, Henry Wadsworth Longfellow and Horace Greeley. Active in the abolitionist movement, Elliott reputedly harbored many fugitive slaves in his cellar. During the Civil War, he organized a volunteer regiment, the Seventy-ninth Highlanders, to fight for the Union. His beautifully proportioned Gothic Revival stone house, built as a real estate investment in 1840 and designated a landmark in 1998, is one of twenty-two designed by Elliott and constructed of locally quarried stone.

ANNA LEONOWENS'S SCHOOL

New Brighton

King Mongkut of Siam (now Thailand) hired Englishwoman Anna Harriet Leonowens to teach his children at the royal court in Bangkok during the 1860s. After leaving the court, Leonowens lived on Tompkins Place from

1868 to 1872 and opened a private school for girls. Known as a literary speaker and as a suffragette, she wrote *The English Governess at the Siamese Court*, dated "New Brighton, Staten Island, September 13, 1872." In it, she thanked neighbor Francis G. Shaw, a women's rights supporter. Her story was later novelized by Margaret Landon as *Anna and the King* (1944) and adapted as Rogers and Hammerstein's musical *The King and I*, which won a Tony Award for best musical in 1952.

UNITARIAN CHURCH OF STATEN ISLAND (LIBRARY)

312 Fillmore Street, New Brighton

Staten Island's Unitarian Church, whose members included literary and social justice movement notables, such as the Curtis and Shaw families, established the Castleton Free Circulating Library. Staten Island's interest in a public library began as early as 1833 when the Franklin Society established a social library in Factoryville (now West New Brighton). The Unitarian Church library still holds many books from the collections of early church members, and "Castleton Free Library" stamps still mark the pages of several titles.

STATEN ISLAND CHILDREN'S MUSEUM

1000 Richmond Terrace, Snug Harbor Cultural Center, New Brighton

The Staten Island Children's Museum grew out of a grass-roots effort by parents in the community to put a world-class cultural resource, designed with children in mind, on Staten Island. After a short period as a "museum without walls," the museum opened its doors in 1976 and relocated to the grounds of Snug Harbor in 1986. The museum has expanded its facility to forty thousand square feet and serves 250,000 people annually.

With its own working farm, bakery and chapel, Sailors' Snug Harbor retirement community was home for up to one thousand "aged, decrepit seamen" in the early 1900s. *Courtesy of Staten Island Museum.*

SAILORS' SNUG HARBOR

1000 Richmond Terrace, New Brighton

SEE THE ARTS, ENVIRONMENT AND ARCHITECTURE

Sailors' Snug Harbor opened in 1833 as a home for "aged, decrepit seamen" under the provisions of a will executed in 1801 for Captain Robert Richard Randall. Snug Harbor was a self-sustaining community comprised of a working farm, dairy, bakery, chapel, hospital and cemetery. During its peak between 1880 and 1910, more than one thousand seamen resided here.

Chapter 3

BUSINESS AND THE ECONOMY

Charles L. Sachs

Contributors: Patrick Donagan, Lori R. Weintrob and Adam Zalma

W hen industrialist Charles W. Hunt and real estate developer Cornelius Kolff organized the Staten Island Chamber of Commerce in 1895, the borough boasted some of the foremost industries in the United States. The chamber's earliest members included bankers, hotel proprietors, brewers, shipbuilders, railroad and utility managers, lawyers, architects, engineers and manufacturers of linoleum, textiles, pencils and fireworks. It was a turning point in the island's economic development.

From the Dutch colonial settlement at Oude Dorp (and prior centuries of Lenape habitation) to the Civil War, Staten Islanders had sustained themselves by farming, fishing, producing handicrafts, milling and trading across the waters of New York Harbor. Even as agriculture, fisheries and shipping continued to engage residents into the twentieth century, a rapidly changing national market economy propelled a steady influx of people—American migrants and foreign immigrants—who brought diverse new skills.

Large-scale manufacturing arrived in 1819 with the opening of the New York Dyeing and Printing Establishment for textiles. A new commercial center, called Factoryville (now West New Brighton), developed around it. Other industries followed: lager beer breweries in Stapleton, Clifton and Castleton Corners; clay mines and brickworks in Kreischerville (Charleston); and the first linoleum factory in America in Linoleumville (Travis). On the New Brighton waterfront, the J.B. King Windsor Plaster Mill was the largest gypsum processing plant in the United States, and in Prince's Bay, S.S.

White Company operated one of the country's largest dental equipment supply factories. Atlantic Terra Cotta Company in Tottenville produced ornament for classic Manhattan skyscrapers and buildings around the world. From 1907 to 1991, Procter and Gamble's huge Port Ivory factory complex employed thousands of men and women.

When local manufacturing declined after World War II, as elsewhere in New York City, commerce and service industries expanded. By the beginning of the twenty-first century, the island's largest private employment areas were in educational and health-related services (more than 34 percent) and retail trades, transportation or utilities (25 percent), followed by jobs in construction, finance, business services and hospitality. Three local banks, an insurance agency and the daily *Staten Island Advance* trace their roots to the 1880s. Many other enterprises have been in business since the 1920s. On Staten Island, entrepreneurship and tradition remain strong.

STATEN ISLAND CHAMBER OF COMMERCE

130 Bay Street, St. George

The Staten Island Chamber of Commerce has been serving merchants and residents since 1895. The chamber's first president was Charles W. Hunt, a national manufacturer of coal-handling machinery. Originally located at 57 Bay Street in the offices of its secretary and fifth president, Cornelius G. Kolff, a real estate developer and local historian, the chamber moved to its present location in 1951. Since its inception, the chamber has provided assistance to thousands of Staten Island businesses, large and small.

THE BREWERIES

Near Tappen Park, Stapleton (Former Site)

German immigrants brought entrepreneurial skills and love of beer to Staten Island. By the 1870s they had established eight breweries producing 160,000 barrels annually, with an estimated value of $1.5 million. The distinctive German lager beer required special yeast, large quantities of fresh water and space for cooling and fermenting, all found here on Staten Island. Bechtel, Bachmann, Eckstein and later Rubsam and Horrmann (R&H) won awards

From the 1880s to the 1960s, local lager beer manufacturers, such as Rubsam & Horrmann Brewing Company, were appreciated around the world. *Photograph by Herbert A. Flamm. Courtesy of Staten Island Historical Society.*

and contracts internationally, shipping beer as far as Paris, Tokyo and Sydney. R&H alone survived Prohibition (1919–1933) by manufacturing cereal beverages, such as malt tonic, with less than 0.5 percent alcohol. R&H lasted until 1953, when Piels Brothers took over the plant and continued operation until January 1963.

Staten Island Savings Bank

81 Water Street, Stapleton

In 1867, Staten Island Savings Bank, the first successful bank in the borough, opened to meet the needs of early industrial expansion. Among its founders were civic leader and abolitionist Francis G. Shaw and brewery owner George Bechtel. It was located in Stapleton's commercial district, first in the Village Hall and then, after 1925, in a landmarked building designed by Delano and Aldrich. As the borough's population expanded, its assets grew from $15 million (1937) to $1 billion (1990). Under the leadership of Harry Doherty, it developed from a mutual to SI Bank and Trust, formed the Staten Island Foundation and, after 2007, was traded on the stock exchange. In 2006, it became part of Sovereign Bancorp.

Free Trade Zone/Home Port

Front Street, Stapleton

In 1920, Mayor John Hylan invested $30 million in the Stapleton waterfront to open new municipal piers. Five piers housed the first Free Trade Zone in the United States from 1937—after Congress passed legislation to stimulate foreign trade—to 1942. West African cocoa beans, Javanese tapioca, Argentine beef, Scandinavian fish oil and, later, Japanese transistor radios were among the forty-five thousand tons of goods stored or exported there annually through the 1970s. During World War II, the United States military used the piers as a port of embarkation, sending troops and supplies to combat theaters overseas. In 1990, the U.S. Navy opened the short-lived home port base there. Fleet Week is celebrated annually at the site.

Wrigley's Chewing Gum/L.A. Dreyfus Factory

Edgewater Street, Rosebank

In 1869, exiled Mexican president Antonio Lopez de Santa Anna introduced chicle, a natural gum from the Central American sapodilla tree, to New York inventor Thomas Adams as a potential rubber substitute. Adams found success, instead, marketing "Adams New York 1," a pure chicle gum, and the licorice-flavored gum "Black Jack." In 1909, Staten Island chemist Dr. Louis A. Dreyfus invented and began to manufacture a synthetic compound for chicle gum, which he sold to, among others, William J. Wrigley Jr.'s Chicago-based company. The L.A. Dreyfus factory operated in Rosebank until moving to Edison, New Jersey, in 1949.

SOUTH BEACH

Father Capodanno Boulevard, South Beach

"If we go on a boat, we dance all the way there and all the way back, and we dance nearly all the time we are there," wrote one young German immigrant to New York about her summer visit to South Beach. *Courtesy of Staten Island Museum.*

On June 30, 1906, thirty thousand people attended the opening day of Happyland Amusement Park, South Beach. Rivaling Coney Island, hotels, beer gardens, a vaudeville theater and a swimming pool attracted visitors, who came by ferry from Manhattan and Brooklyn directly to the piers. One German immigrant wrote in 1903: "If we go on a boat, we dance all the way there and all the way back, and we dance nearly all the time we are there." A popular destination since the 1880s, fires in 1917 and 1929, along with pollution from sewage and oil, made the water unsafe for swimming. In 1935, Works Progress Administration (WPA) funding helped build the Franklin Delano Roosevelt Boardwalk. Smaller amusement parks lasted until 2006. Today, South Beach and its boardwalk are once again a popular destination.

1199 SERVICE EMPLOYEES INTERNATIONAL UNION

1282 Richmond Road, Dongan Hills

Labor unions have existed on Staten Island since the nineteenth century, among them the Order of United American Mechanics. The borough was also birthplace of national labor leader Ella Reeve Bloor, who assisted Upton

Sinclair, a fellow member of the Socialist Party of America, in gathering information about Chicago's meatpacking industry for his book *The Jungle*. Although strikes were more common before World War II, unions remain an important presence in the borough. Among them, branch 1199 of the 250,000-member Service Employees International Union represents healthcare, public service and property service workers.

STATWOOD HOME IMPROVEMENTS

1475 Hylan Boulevard, Dongan Hills

Founded in 1925, Statwood Home Improvements continues as a leading home improvement contractor under the direction of Michael Kraus, the third-generation owner. It joined the Staten Island Chamber of Commerce in 1930 and has been at its present location for over forty years.

STATEN ISLAND ADVANCE

950 Fingerboard Road, Grasmere

John Crawford and James Kennedy first published the *Richmond County Advance* as a four-page weekly newspaper on March 27, 1886, one of nine newspapers on the island. In 1918, it was published daily at 1267 Castleton Avenue, West New Brighton, and renamed the *Daily Advance*.

The J.J. Crawford Print Shop in 1894, publisher of the *Richmond County Advance*, later renamed the *Staten Island Advance. Courtesy of* Staten Island Advance. All Rights Reserved.

Samuel Irving Newhouse, son of Jewish-Russian immigrants, purchased the *Staten Island Advance* in 1922, a step in building his media empire. His nephew, Richard E. Diamond, oversaw publication, technological improvements and civic endeavors for five decades. Diamond's daughter, Caroline Diamond Harrison, succeeded him as publisher. The *Staten Island Advance* is the only remaining major daily published in a borough outside Manhattan.

"STATEN ISLAND ADVANCE AT 125"

Brian J. Laline, Editor

Hello, Staten Island!

All of us at the *Staten Island Advance* are very excited. The town we love is celebrating its 350th birthday, and the newspaper that chronicles the happenings here every day is celebrating its 125th anniversary—all in the same year!

We are proud to call Staten Island home, and we are proud to bring news and advertising that's important to our readers seven days a week, both in print and on the Internet at silive.com. The *Advance* is the best place to find out what's happening in our community.

So much has changed on Staten Island during the past 25 or 50 years. Imagine how much has changed in the *Advance*'s 125 years or the 350 years our community has existed. Where once Staten Island farmers tilled the soil, there are now thousands of homes. Where horse and buggies once traveled our roadways, now thousands and thousands of cars do the same.

Yet we manage to retain a small-town atmosphere in the greenest borough of any in New York City. The late *Advance* publisher Richard E. Diamond, who loved Staten Island, put it perfectly: "Staten Island," he said, "is a borough of small towns." Indeed, Staten Island is the best place to live in New York!

And we are a town rich in history: the Conference House; Snug Harbor Cultural Center; Historic Richmond Town; Fort Wadsworth; stunning architecture on our North Shore; and the wonderful beaches, fields and forests on our South and East Shores. What was once the largest landfill on the planet soon will be the gem of the West Shore, as it takes shape into what will be New York City's grandest park for our children and grandchildren.

What's so exiting as we celebrate 350 years is how the fabric of our community is changing. New neighbors from all over the world are meeting each other as our population swells. They are bringing new businesses, restaurants and cultural experiences for all to enjoy, expanding Staten Island's horizons and enriching everyone's lives.

The *Advance* salutes Staten Island and Staten Islanders at this unique and exciting time in our history. Congratulations, all!

THE STATEN ISLAND MALL

2655 Richmond Avenue, New Springville

Once site of the Staten Island Airport, the Staten Island Mall traces its origins back to 1964 when airport operator Edward McCormick lost his lease, and the property owner sold the land. The mall opened for business nine years later on August 9, 1973. Now owned by General Growth Properties, Inc., and anchored by Macy's, Sears and J.C. Penney, the mall has two hundred stores and kiosks, with thirty thousand employees, and hosts seasonal events featuring Santa Claus and the Easter Bunny, as well as community programs.

SANDY GROUND

1538 Woodrow Road, Rossville

SEE ALSO ARCHITECTURE

After slavery was abolished in New York in 1827, free blacks migrated to this area where sandy soil proved conducive to strawberry farming. Free black oystermen from Snow Hill, Maryland, fleeing discriminatory laws, joined the original settlers, such as the Harris brothers. First known as Harrisville and then Little Africa, this South Shore community became a safe haven for African Americans. In the late nineteenth century, the thriving community included craftsmen and business owners. New York state closed the oyster beds in the 1920s, as pollution worsened in the bay. Many residents drifted away in subsequent decades. By the twenty-first century, grass-roots efforts and the community's unique history have brought it renewed interest and efforts to preserve its history.

Sandy Ground Quilters Circle has used traditional handicraft to pay homage to the contributions of African Americans to New York City and American history. This quilt memorializes the African American strawberry farmers who settled here, alongside oystermen and craftsmen in the 1830s. *Courtesy of Sandy Ground Historical Society and former Congressman Michael McMahon's office.*

S.S. WHITE DENTAL MANUFACTURING COMPANY

Seguine Avenue, Prince's Bay

In 1927, with almost two thousand male and female employees, S.S. White was the largest employer on Staten Island, manufacturing dental equipment and supplies. S.S. White was created in 1881 when a Staten Island company owned by Algernon Johnston and his brothers merged with a large Philadelphia-based firm established by Dr. Samuel Stockton White. The site in Prince's Bay, once used for candle making, was converted in 1865 to create the "factory by the sea." Acquired by Pennwalt in 1968, the company moved to New Jersey in 1972.

ATLANTIC TERRA COTTA

Ellis Street, Tottenville (Former Site)

Atlantic Terra Cotta, on North Broadway (today's Ellis Street), designed and manufactured architectural fabric and ornaments for prestigious early skyscrapers, such as the Flatiron Building and the Woolworth Building (1913) in Manhattan, as well as the Philadelphia Museum of Art. From its 1897 founding to 1932, its five hundred laborers and skilled craftsmen—often immigrants from Germany, Italy or Eastern Europe—made products shipped around the world. The use of fire-resistant terra cotta, literally "cooked earth," was a response to the disastrous urban fires of Chicago (1871) and Boston (1872).

Atlantic Terra Cotta, Tottenville, designed ornamentation for prestigious early skyscrapers such as the Flatiron Building and the Woolworth Building (1913) in Manhattan. *Courtesy of Staten Island Historical Society.*

Tottenville Copper Company/Nassau Smelting

Nassau Place, Tottenville

Benjamin Lowenstein, a New York metals merchant, began the Tottenville Copper Company in 1900, refining various metals, including copper and lead. In 1931, Western Electric, the manufacturing arm for Bell Telephone, combined the plant with Nassau Smelting and Refining. It became the major salvage operation for Bell, recovering various metals from old equipment and wires. With the breakup of the Bell System and then AT&T, the property became part of Lucent Technologies. Lucent repositioned the facility as its Electroplating Chemicals and Services subsidiary, opening new chemical and material diagnostic and analytic laboratories in 1999. Amid restructuring, Lucent closed the site.

Port Mobil (Kinder Morgan Liquids Terminals)

4101 Arthur Kill Road, Charleston

Originally called Port Socony, the Port Mobil Terminal, on the southwestern corner of the borough, is a 203-acre petroleum storage and distribution facility dating to 1934. Thirty-nine above-ground tanks hold 125 million gallons of gasoline, jet fuel and home heating oil. In 1999, Mobil and Exxon merged; two years later, after a lawsuit, Exxon Mobil Corp. was ordered to restore environmentally sensitive land on the Arthur Kill. In 2003, a gas barge exploded at the terminal, killing two crewmen. Since 2005, Kinder Morgan Energy Partners, LP, has operated it. Port Mobil is also the oldest archaeological site in New York City, where significant evidence of Paleo-Indian settlement (eleven thousand years ago) has been discovered.

Kreischer Brick Factory and Worker Housing

71 Kreischer Street, Charleston

In 1854, twenty years after settling in Manhattan, German-born Balthazar Kreischer established a brick factory and clay mines on the Arthur Kill. By the late 1890s, Kreischer and Sons turned out 3.5 million bricks yearly that were used throughout the metropolitan area and are still visible on Kreischer Street. Clay came from rich deposits nearby, including today's Clay Pit Ponds State Park Preserve. Much like the Steinway family, piano manufacturers in Astoria, Queens, Kreischer hired German immigrant workers and built a Lutheran church and still-standing worker housing, both of which are New York City landmarks. The area, once known as Androvetteville and today Charleston, was named in his honor.

LINOLEUMVILLE (NOW TRAVIS)

The first linoleum factory in America opened here in 1874, along the shores of the Arthur Kill. Linoleum's British inventor, Francis Walton, named the inexpensive, mass-produced, ornamental floor covering for its primary ingredient, linseed oil. Walton came to Staten Island to supervise the construction of the three-hundred-acre American Linoleum Manufacturing Company facility, which included docking facilities, workers' cottages and factories. Workers came at first from Britain and Scotland, but by the firm's apex in 1910, many of its seven hundred male and female employees—who produced ninety thousand square yards per week—were from Germany, Hungary and elsewhere in Eastern Europe. In 1931, competition led to its shutdown, just shortly after the town was renamed Travis.

Some of the seven hundred American Linoleum Company's workers, largely immigrants from Scotland, England, Germany and Hungary, enjoy a noon break at the Linoleumville factory circa 1900 (now Travis). *Courtesy of Staten Island Historical Society.*

ARTHUR KILL GENERATING STATION (NRG ENERGY, INC.)

4401 Victory Boulevard, Travis

In 1887, Edison Electric Illuminating Company first provided street lighting on Staten Island. The first use of electricity was at the American Linoleum

Manufacturing Plant, Travis. Many small companies were consolidated into the New York and Staten Island Electric Company, with a central power plant in Livingston (1897–1963). From 1902 to 1923, Richmond Light and Railroad Company managed both electricity and electric trolleys until taken over by the Staten Island Edison Corporation. Consolidated Edison purchased the company in 1952. The Arthur Kill power plant opened in 1947 and was expanded in 1959. It was transferred by Con Edison to NRG Energy Inc. in 1999.

STATEN ISLAND CORPORATE PARK

900–1150 South Avenue, Bloomfield

Four important Staten Island businesses call South Avenue home: the Staten Island Economic Development Corporation (SIEDC), the Nicotra Group, Supreme Chocolatier and the Teleport. Since 1993, SIEDC has served as an economic advocate for Staten Island's business community, introducing over $550 million in new investments and over 3,500 jobs into the economy. The Nicotra Group, founded in 1976, owns, manages and leases nearly 1,000,000 square feet of commercial space located within a 415-acre wildlife preserve. The Katsoris family is responsible for Supreme Chocolatier, a Staten Island chocolate producer founded in 1911. The Teleport contains Telehouse, a data backup company with international connections.

RUSSO-PICCIURRO-MALOY INSURANCE

1000 South Avenue, Bloomfield

The Russo-Picciurro-Maloy (RPM) Insurance Agency, the largest independent insurance agency on Staten Island, serves thousands of clients in the metropolitan area with life, business and health insurance. Mark Russo, RPM's director, is the third generation to direct Russo Agency, founded in 1926 by his grandfather, James, son of Italian immigrants. Mark's maternal great-great-grandfather, Charles Griffith, founded a real estate and insurance agency in 1886. The Griffith Building, once a business hub, still stands at the corner of Richmond Terrace and Port Richmond Avenue. RPM traces its roots to 1872, when the Maloy Agency Inc. was founded; it was acquired in 1999 by Russo-Picciurro Agency, LLC.

PROCTER AND GAMBLE

Western Avenue, Port Ivory (Former Site)

In 1907, on 77 acres in Port Ivory, the commercial soap-making firm of Procter and Gamble (P&G) began producing one million cases per year of Ivory and Lenox bar soap. William Procter and James Gamble, English and Irish immigrants respectively, founded P&G in 1837 in Cincinnati, Ohio, and rose to prominence after the 1879 development of Ivory soap. By the late 1920s, 1,500 men and women worked on the Port Ivory production line, creating soap bars and chips, Crisco shortening and "oil meal" for animal feed in twenty-eight buildings on 129 acres. One of only two large manufacturing establishments left on Staten Island by 1980, it closed in 1991.

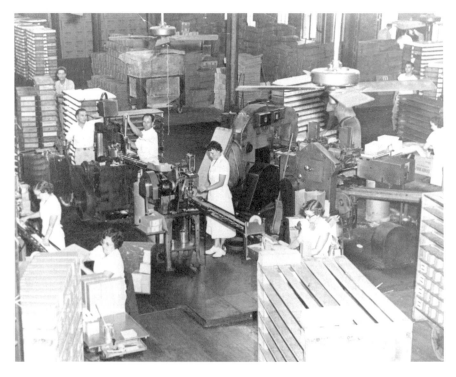

At Procter and Gamble's Port Ivory factory, on October 8, 1954, men and women are cutting, stamping, wrapping and packing Ivory soap. *Courtesy of Staten Island Historical Society.*

NEW YORK CONTAINER TERMINAL, INC. (NYCT)

40 Western Avenue, Howland Hook

By the mid-1960s, a new technique called containerization, pioneered by the Port Authority in Ports Newark and Elizabeth but absent from New York City, dominated international shipping. Jakob Isbrandtsen, owner of American Export–Isbrandtsen Lines, proposed the Howland Hook container terminal in 1966. Purchased by New York City shortly after it opened in 1972, the facility remained underused until the 1990s. The resurgence of freight shipping today has brought dramatically higher volumes to the site. With a staff of 1,100 in 2009, NYCT, Inc., was the largest private employer on the island's North Shore. Just below the Goethals Bridge is the former Gulfport, where, in 1928, the Gulf Refining Company purchased land and constructed more than one hundred tanks used in the storage and transportation of oil until 1999.

PORT RICHMOND BUSINESS DISTRICT

Port Richmond Avenue

The original "downtown" of Staten Island, in 1838, Richard Littell founded the first bank on Staten Island here, down the block from the St. James Hotel, where former vice president Aaron Burr died. Across the street, the Jewett White Lead Company, founded in 1842, produced 3,500 tons of white lead annually. A center of manufacturing and shipbuilding until World War II, the area's local firms employed hundreds of workers from Ireland, Germany and Scandinavia. To serve these workers, a business district developed called the "Fifth Avenue" of Staten Island, with three theaters, restaurants and retail shops, such as Woolworths, Garber Brothers, Tirone's Shoes and Lobel's. Commercial activity declined by the 1970s, but recently it has been reinvigorated by long-standing local organizations and a new wave of immigrants.

"COMMODORE" CORNELIUS VANDERBILT'S BIRTHPLACE

Faber Park Vicinity, Port Richmond

In 1715, Jacob Van Derbilt and Nelje Denyse moved from Manhattan to a Staten Island farm. Their grandson, Cornelius, a ferryboat operator,

"Commodore" Cornelius Vanderbilt, born in Port Richmond, operated an early steam ferry from Vanderbilt's Landing (now Clifton) to Manhattan. *Courtesy of Staten Island Museum.*

married New Jersey native Phebe Hand. In 1791, they purchased a farmhouse in Port Richmond, where their fourth son, Cornelius—the future "Commodore" (1794–1877)—was born. The family moved to a larger house in Stapleton, but young Cornelius returned to farm this acre and earned $100 to purchase his first ferryboat. He went on to make a legendary fortune in shipping and railroads. In the 1890s, lead pencil manufacturer and German immigrant Eberhard Faber built his home on this waterfront area, which later became Faber Park.

FARRELL LUMBER

2076 Richmond Terrace, Port Richmond (Former Site)

In 1900, Harry S. Farrell arrived from New Jersey and took over Conklin Mills, founded in 1888. Farrell Lumber provided chestnut, pine and other wood purchased from as far away as China and California to craft the moldings and doors in thousands of homes in New York and New Jersey. It contributed wood for barrels for overseas shipping during World War II and supplied over 100,000 feet of lumber for the Verrazano-Narrows Bridge. The family business closed in 2009.

RICHMOND COUNTY SAVINGS BANK

1207 Castleton Avenue, West New Brighton (and Other Branches)

Founded on October 20, 1886, Richmond County Savings Bank had as its first president local businessman and German immigrant Monroe Eckstein, owner of Eckstein's Brewery. It was located on Richmond

---

RICHMOND COUNTY SAVINGS FOUNDATION

900 South Avenue, Executive Suite 17, Bloomfield

In 1998, Richmond County Savings Bank created the Richmond County Savings Foundation as a legacy to the Staten Island community. Richmond County Savings Foundation is committed to its mission of providing support for the programs and services of charitable and nonprofit organizations, which advance educational opportunity, enrich cultural development and strengthen health and human services.

Richmond County Savings Foundation has become a leading philanthropic institution in the Staten Island community and beyond. This year, the foundation funded a program to support food pantries islandwide that will provide food to thousands. Richmond County Savings Foundation has also been a partner in many capital projects throughout the island, including Staten Island University Hospital's Adult Emergency Trauma Center and Foundation Hall at Wagner College.

The continued success of the Richmond County Savings Bank, a division of New York Community Bank, enables the foundation to invest in Staten Island communities through worthy nonprofit organizations. To date, the foundation has contributed over $42 million in a continuation of the bank's role as a proactive community partner.

Terrace in New Brighton at the Odd Fellows Building. In 1998, with $1 billion in assets, it converted to a publicly traded company under the leadership of President Michael F. Manzulli. In addition, the Richmond County Savings Bank Foundation was created, and it has since donated over $42 million to the community. In 2001, Richmond County Savings Bank merged with Queens County Savings Bank and became part of New York Community Bancorp, Inc., which today is the twenty-third largest bank-holding company in the nation.

FACTORYVILLE/CHARLES GOODYEAR

West New Brighton

Large-scale manufacturing arrived on Staten Island in 1819 when Massachusetts-born entrepreneurs opened Barrett, Tileston and Company (later, New York Dyeing and Printing Establishment) for textiles. A new commercial center, called Factoryville, developed around it. Connecticut-born inventor and businessman Charles Goodyear established a factory here in 1835 to produce clothing, life preservers, shoes and other goods made with Indian rubber. After the Panic of 1837, he moved to Massachusetts, where, three years later, he discovered that heating natural rubber and sulfur created vulcanized rubber. Factoryville was renamed West New Brighton about 1870.

C.W. HUNT COAL HANDLING MACHINERY

West New Brighton (Former Site)

In 1868, engineer and inventor Charles W. Hunt came to Staten Island and established a retail coal business, which evolved into a national coal-machinery manufacturing enterprise. His inventions, which led to the acquisition of 147 patents, were installed in most American ports and U.S. Navy coaling stations. Coal had been unloaded by hand from barges or railroad cars until Hunt invented the grab (or "clam-shell") bucket, automatic railway cranes, the pivotal bucket carrier and many other devices operated by steam engines. In 1895, he helped found and served as first president of the Staten Island Chamber of Commerce.

WIESNER BROS. NURSERY

2402 Victory Boulevard, Willowbrook

Established in 1928, Wiesner Bros. Nursery has grown to become the largest retail nursery in New York City. Cofounded by German immigrants from Silbitz, Max Wiesner and his brother, the business was passed down to Max's son, Ralph Sr., in 1967. It has since been handed to the third generation, nurseryman Ralph Jr. and landscape architect Hans.

ATLANTIC SALT COMPANY/U.S. GYPSUM

561 Richmond Terrace, New Brighton

In 1876, J.B. King and Company's Windsor Plaster Mill opened on this ten-acre waterfront site and quickly dominated the plaster business on the Atlantic coast. Purchased by the Chicago-based U.S. Gypsum Corporation, its five hundred employees made sheetrock, plaster, paint and other products from 1924 to 1973. Family-owned Atlantic Salt, which supplies salt for deicing roadways throughout the region, acquired the site in 1977. Salt from around the world is received at its marine terminal. In 2010, Mayor Michael Bloomberg recognized Atlantic Salt with the NYC Small Business of the Year Award.

HOTEL CASTLETON

St. Marks Place, New Brighton (Former Site)

By the 1840s, Staten Island's shorefront and village hotels drew wealthy visitors from around the world, especially in the summertime. At 125 St. Marks Place, the four-hundred-room St. Mark's Hotel (built in 1876) was replaced by the grander Hotel Castleton in 1889. The hotel was a popular, elegant destination until destroyed by fire in 1907, contributing to the decline in local resort business caused by pollution. The site is now occupied by the cooperative Castleton Park Apartments.

Hotel Castleton, the grandest of several elegant hotels in New Brighton with views of New York Harbor, was built in 1889 and destroyed by fire in 1907. *Courtesy of Staten Island Museum.*

Chapter 4

ETHNICITY AND IMMIGRATION

Christopher Mulé and Lori R. Weintrob

Contributors: Bonnie McCourt, Andrew Wilson and Hesham El-Meligy

In 1710, a Staten Island schoolteacher observed that the population represented "all the nations under heaven." A mix of Dutch, Belgian, French and Africans populated Oude Dorp, Dutch for Old Town. Huguenots (French Protestants), memorialized in the town of that name, were the island's first religious refugees. Few original inhabitants, the Native American Lenape, a diverse group of Raritan, Hackensack and Canarsie tribes, remained. Only gradually after the British takeover of "Statten Eylandt" in 1664 did the English arrive and intermarry.

Many families owned one or two enslaved Africans, who accounted for 20 percent of the island's population. The American Revolution brought occupation by thirty-two thousand British troops, Hessian (German) allies and African American Loyalists fighting for their freedom. In 1827, emancipation became law in New York state. Free black oystermen from Maryland and Virginia joined newly free local black farmers to found a community at Sandy Ground.

In the 1830s, on the eve of the Great Potato Famine, Irish and German immigrants flocked to Staten Island's shores. Some passed through the quarantine located here from 1799 to 1858. These newcomers, notably Catholics, were not welcomed by all. Yet as workers or employers, in the Kreisherville brickworks, beer breweries and shops, they established churches, singing clubs and shooting societies and gradually entered political life.

The development of shipyards and the 1893 European economic crisis drew laborers from Scandinavia, Poland, Hungary and Italy. Eastern

European Jews, peddlers at first, opened stores in Port Richmond and Stapleton. By the 1920s, Greek farmers were hard at work along Richmond Avenue. Anti-immigrant feelings around the country led to the 1924 National Quota Law that slowed immigration. In 1965, as part of the civil rights movement, ethnic quotas were lifted, and those from Africa, Asia and Latin America again flocked to the island.

Chinese immigrants, present on Staten Island since the early 1900s, established the Chinese-American Club of Staten Island in 1970. By the 1980s, many Filipinos, Syrians and Mexicans, along with Russian and Ukranian Jewish refugees, sought economic opportunities here. Amid devastating civil wars in the 1990s, Liberians and Sri Lankans arrived in great numbers. In 2010, one-fifth of Staten Island's inhabitants were born outside the United States. The borough has the fastest-growing immigrant population in the city.

LITTLE SRI LANKA

Victory Boulevard and Cebra Avenue, Tompkinsville

As a result of a civil war in the 1990s, Staten Island became home to five thousand Sri Lankans, more than a third of New York's Sri Lankan population and the third-largest Sri Lankan community outside of the mother country. While there are ethnic clashes there, Tamils and Sinhalese are at peace in this Staten Island neighborhood, dubbed Little Sri Lanka. The area is packed with Sri Lankan restaurants, including San Rasa, Dosa Garden and New Asha. Sri Lanka Grocery, Grocery Lanka and New Parkland Grocery sell imported spices, food, newspapers in Sinahlese and Tamil and music.

ALBANIAN ISLAMIC CULTURAL CENTER

307 Victory Boulevard, Tompkinsville

The first Islamic center in Staten Island, Islamic Mesjid of Staten Island, was established in 1973. On September 16, 1990, the Islamic Center relocated to the Albanian Islamic Cultural Center (AICC) on Victory Boulevard. The AICC is a three-floor, forty-thousand-square-foot structure that features a one-hundred-foot minaret, a tower from which the muezzin calls the people to prayer. The center also houses a cultural center, elementary school, mosque and meeting place for more than two thousand Albanian and other Muslims on the island. The vast majority of the Albanian community arrived in the United States during the Communist era and often came via Egypt, Turkey or elsewhere in the Middle East.

St. Stanislaus Kostka Parish

109 York Avenue, New Brighton

In 1901, in the basement of the parish hall of St. Mary's Church, Port Richmond, Father Michael Slupek offered the first Mass for the Poles in Staten Island. When St. Stanislaus Kostka Parish was founded in 1923, it was the borough's third Polish place of worship, after St. Adalbert's of Elm Park (1901) and St. Anthony Parish of Linoleumville, now Travis (1907). Notable pastors have included the Reverend John A. Gloss and the Reverend Stanislaus Malinowski. About twenty thousand Polish families live on Staten Island; newer arrivals from Little Warsaw (Greenpoint, Brooklyn) still greet each other in Polish, with "dobrze" (good). Many also frequent the Polish Place Café and Grocery, 19 Corsen Avenue.

Tappen Park

Canal and Bay Streets, Stapleton

Taking advantage of nearby spring water, Stapleton became famous for its internationally acclaimed breweries founded by German immigrants. In 1867, the town, then known as Edgewater, purchased this property for public use as Washington Square, building in 1889 a brick Village Hall that still stands. In 1934, Mayor Fiorello La Guardia renamed this park in honor of James J. Tappen, who was killed in France during World War I. The local American Legion post was also named in his honor. The Partnerships for Parks now sponsors an annual Oktoberfest with authentic German food and a traditional German oompah band.

German immigration to Staten Island contributed significantly to the island's workforce and reshaped popular culture. *Photograph by George Bear. Courtesy of Staten Island Museum.*

CHRIST ASSEMBLY/AFRICAN IMMIGRANT MINISTRY

27 Hudson Street, Stapleton

Civil war and the consequent displacements have brought over 120,000 African immigrants to New York City over the past twenty years. Liberians are among the most well established of the 25,000 Africans in the borough, also home to a diverse population from Nigeria, Senegal, Sierra Leone and Ghana. Since 1996, the Christ Assembly/African Immigrant Ministry has provided outreach education, citizenship classes and interfaith and transnational fellowship. Founder Father Philip Saywrayne highlights "the high value that Africans put on education, as well as networking with the community, including others of African descent."

THE STATEN ISLAND LIBERIAN COMMUNITY ASSOCIATION (SILCA)

180 Park Hill Avenue, Clifton

Founded in 1984, the Staten Island Liberian Community Association (SILCA) serves the interests of the estimated ten thousand Liberians and people of Liberian descent on Staten Island. SILCA has aided in the shipment of relief items, especially food, medical supplies and financial assistance, to displacement centers in Liberia and refugee camps in critical areas in West Africa, such as Ghana, Guinea, Sierra Leone and Ivory Coast. On July 30, 2010, borough president James P. Molinaro read an official proclamation endorsing the celebration of Liberia's 163rd Independence Day. SILCA president Telee Brown called for "clear and concrete interaction between home-based and Diaspora Liberians."

MASJID AL-NOOR/MUSLIM MAJLIS OF STATEN ISLAND

SEE RELIGION

PHIL-AM FOOD MART

SEE FOOD AND DRINK

GARIBALDI-MEUCCI MUSEUM

420 Tompkins Avenue, Rosebank

This Gothic Revival cottage was the home of Antonio Meucci, the true inventor of the telephone. In the early 1850s, Meucci offered refuge in the house to Giuseppe Garibaldi, the legendary hero who championed the unification of Italy. In 1906, the house was moved to its current location, and a large pantheon was erected over it, creating the Garibaldi

"Throngs from Little Italies to Patriot's House of Exile on Staten Island," read the *New York Times* headline after ten thousand visitors dedicated the Garibaldi Memorial in 1907. *Courtesy of Garibaldi-Meucci Museum.*

Memorial. In the early 1950s, the pantheon was dismantled, and the building was opened as a museum. For over fifty years, the museum has preserved the legacies of these men and promoted understanding of the Italian American heritage through cultural, artistic and educational programs.

OUDE DORP

Arrochar

The first permanent settlers of Staten Island—with a deed signed on August 22, 1661, by the director general of New Netherlands, Peter Stuyvesant—built their homes in Oude Dorp (Old Town in Dutch) on the banks of a creek, now disappeared. Pierre Billiou (of the Billiou-Stillwell-Perine House), a French-speaking Protestant (Walloon) from the southern Netherlands (today's Belgium), was the first sheriff. Like Billiou, the majority of French colonists were Huguenots and Walloons escaping religious persecution in their native countries. Located in present-day South Beach, Oude Dorp was renamed Dover when New Amsterdam was turned over to the English by the Dutch—initially in 1664 and permanently in 1674—and renamed New York. By 1695, the population of 727 on the island was divided equally between Dutch, French/Belgian and English, with 70 enslaved Africans sharing the labor.

TURKISH CULTURAL CENTER STATEN ISLAND (TCCSI)

1756 Hylan Boulevard, Dongan Hills

The Turkish Cultural Center has five centers in the metropolitan area. In 2009, a branch opened in Dongan Hills to serve Staten Island's five-hundred-person Turkish-American community and sponsor education and cultural programs, promote intercultural dialogue and educate Staten Islanders about Turkey's unique heritage. Mehmet Kilic, the president of the TCCSI, emphasizes that, "for the Turkish community, the United States is more than a land of freedom of opportunity; it is a country of diversity; it's a country of peace, tolerance, dialogue and acceptance."

STATEN ISLAND COMMUNITY CENTER

219 Jefferson Avenue, Dongan Hills

An estimated 5 percent of Staten Island's 2010 population arrived from Russia, Ukraine and other lands of the former Soviet Union. Over half are college educated, and many own shops, beauty salons, restaurants or media companies. Ukrainian entrepreneur Arkadiy Fridman started the Staten Island Community Center to "combine Russian culture with American culture and create something better" to serve a multicultural population in the borough. The center runs a day-care center and other events, such as family festivals. A first wave of Russian Jews (late 1800s) and their descendants has made an impact on Staten Island as well.

CENTER FOR MIGRATION STUDIES

209 Flagg Place, Todt Hill

The Center for Migration Studies (CMS) was founded in 1964 to collect and disseminate information on international migration. To carry out its mission, CMS publishes *International Migration Review*, the flagship scholarly quarterly in its field, holds conferences on immigration issues and maintains an archive of more than one hundred processed collections documenting the immigrant experience, especially of Italians. CMS is housed in the estate that architect Ernest Flagg built for his Staten Island bride.

Joan and Alan Bernikow Jewish Community Center (JCC)

1466 Manor Road, Manor Heights

The 1927 groundbreaking for the Jewish Community Center (JCC) of Staten Island, with Max Levy, first president of the JCC Board of Directors. *Courtesy of Joan & Alan Bernikow Jewish Community Center.*

When the Jewish Community Center of Staten Island opened its beautiful bronze doors on Victory Boulevard in 1929, it became a home for the Jewish community for social, recreational and educational activities. The JCC's growth paralleled that of the borough: from the North Shore to the South and then to mid-island, from day camp (1932), preschool (1960) and the Dorothy Delson Music Institute to Kosher Meals for the Homebound Elderly and First Foot Forward, a preschool for children with special needs. *L'dor v'dor*—from generation to generation—the JCC thrives today as a center for the Jewish community and a community center for all.

United Hebrew Cemetery/ Mount Richmond Cemetery

122 Arthur Kill Road, Richmond

The Hebrew Free Burial Society (HFBS) purchased Mount Richmond Cemetery in 1909 for New York's indigent Jewish community. Twenty-one young immigrant Jewish women who perished in the 1911 Triangle Shirtwaist Factory fire are buried here. One grave is dedicated to a woman who "never had a chance to grow." Half of the sixty thousand Jews buried here are immigrants, many from Eastern Europe, including the former mayor of Jersey City, New Jersey, Charles Krieger (1914–1982). Mount Richmond Cemetery is adjacent to United Hebrew Cemetery, the final resting place of forty thousand Jewish Americans. Their graves are marked in Hebrew, Yiddish, Russian and English. In acts of vandalism, tombs were desecrated at these sites in 1937, 1952 and 1976.

COPTIC ORTHODOX CHURCH OF ARCHANGEL MICHAEL AND SAINT MENA
SEE RELIGION

MEMORIAL CHURCH OF THE HUGUENOTS
SEE ARCHITECTURE

STATEN ISLAND KOREAN SEVENTH-DAY ADVENTIST CHURCH

940 Huguenot Avenue, Arden Heights

During the 1990s, the Asian population on Staten Island grew by 65 percent, reaching 27,740. The Korean population, estimated at 5,246 in 2007, is the third-largest Asian ethnic group on Staten Island. Many Koreans list church as the most important place to form friendships and find refuge from the strains of immigration-related adjustments. The Staten Island Korean Seventh-Day Adventist Church has a worship service spoken in Korean with Pastor Byung Ho Kim.

GRACE CHRISTIAN CHURCH

991 Woodrow Road, Woodrow

In 1983, a Bible study group comprised of Taiwanese immigrant families became Grace Christian Church (GCC). Under the leadership of Pastor John Chang of Taiwan, they joined the Reformed Church of America (RCA). From 1992 to 1996, the congregation met in the Huguenot Reformed Church until their new place of worship at 991 Woodrow Road opened. Over the past twenty-five years, more than a thousand people were welcomed into the church. An active youth ministry serves overseas in summer camps in Taiwan and China. Grace Christian Church now has services in English, Mandarin and Taiwanese.

SANDY GROUND
SEE ARCHITECTURE AND BUSINESS AND THE ECONOMY

MAGYAR (HUNGARIAN) REFORMED CHURCH
SEE RELIGION

WARD'S POINT ARCHAEOLOGICAL SITE

Conference House Park, Tottenville

SEE ALSO RELIGION

This Lenape stone head sculpture, found near Fingerboard Road in 1884, testifies to Native American art on the island and its appreciation by early collectors at the Staten Island Museum, where it is on display. Similar sculptures have been found in Pennsylvania, suggesting travel and other ties between various Native American groups. *Courtesy of Staten Island Museum.*

Ward's Point is the largest, best-preserved and most intensively studied archaeological locale associated with Native Americans in the metropolitan New York area. Artifacts chronicle contact between Munsee-speaking Lenape people and Europeans during the seventeenth century. Knowledge of the site dates back to 1858, when workmen excavating the foundations of a house unearthed the first-reported human interments. Part of Conference House Park, this national landmark was named for the family of Caleb Ward who lived here after the American Revolution. Alaska Street, Richmond Terrace and Wolfe's Pond Park are among the many other sites testifying to a Native American presence dating back to 1100.

ASIAN FOOD MARKET

1801 South Avenue, Travis

About 8 percent of borough residents are Asian. Asian Food Market features a wide selection of Asian groceries from many regions of China, Taiwan, the Philippines, Japan, Korea, India and several southeastern Asian countries, as well as educational programs about Chinese holidays. Favorite items include garlic-scallion chicken and Filipino crisp deep-fried spare ribs and roasted pig for big celebrations. This store is one of six opened by W.K. Chan since 1992.

NANSEN LODGE

3441 Victory Boulevard, Bull's Head

Since the 1850s, the Norwegians have contributed to the maritime culture of New York City. They worked in the borough's shipyards, notably in Port Richmond. Nansen Lodge, located on nine beautiful acres and organized in 1938, is a fraternal organization affiliated with the Sons of Norway. It promotes an appreciation of the heritage and culture of Norway and other Scandinavian countries. Nansen Lodge offers language classes, folk dancing, a chorus and a junior lodge.

GREEK FARMS

Richmond Avenue, Bull's Head

In the early twentieth century, many Greek farmers came to Staten Island to escape oppression on Lemnos and other disputed territorial islands in the Aegean Sea between Greece and Turkey. Proximity to the markets in Manhattan made the borough a prime farming location. The farms provided seasonal work to Greeks and others, including the poet Langston Hughes, who wrote of his experience on the Criaris farm in 1922. Other Greek families settled in Port Richmond. The foundation of Holy Trinity/ St. Nicholas Greek Orthodox Church was dug with the help of horses from the Greek farms. By the 1960s, depleted soil and housing developments put an end to agricultural activities, although Historic Richmond Town's Decker Farm, once farmed by the Anagnostis family, remains.

Nigerian-American Community Association

295 Granite Avenue, Mariners Harbor

Nigerians and Ghanaians are among the top twenty immigrant groups coming to New York in the twenty-first century. On Staten Island, the Nigerian-American Community Association is part of a national organization that ensures respect for Nigerians in America, alleviates economic and emotional suffering and commemorates Nigerian Independence Day every October. Masjid Rahmatillaah, a religious organization that was founded July 4, 1993, on 36 Hardy Street, Clifton, serves the Nigerian Muslim community. Since the early 1990s, African immigration to Staten Island, including those from Liberia, Ghana, Sierra Leone and Senegal—mostly living on the North Shore—is estimated at twenty-five thousand.

El Centro del Immigrante

1564 Castleton Avenue, Port Richmond

El Centro was opened in 1997 to address the needs of immigrant day laborers and their families, thousands of whom have arrived on Staten Island from Mexico and Latin America since 1990. Project Hospitality, the Latino Civic Association and St. Mary's of the Assumption Church collaborated to form this family center. It has created "a space where recently arrived immigrants can form friendships, receive information and training and make their own contribution to the Staten Island community." Services include English as a Second Language, GED and literacy classes; after-school tutoring; labor organizing; health education and screenings; family and immigrant rights services; immigration counseling; legal assistance; social activities; food and clothing distribution; and community service.

Traditional dance group Latino Folklorico of El Centro del Inmigrante performs at the Cinco de Mayo festival at Faber Park, Port Richmond, in 2010. *Courtesy of Christopher Mulé.*

ALBA HOUSE

2187 Victory Boulevard, Westerleigh

Alba House, a Catholic publishing house run by the Society of St. Vincent de Paul, serves as a meeting site for the John D. Kearney division of the Ancient Order of Hibernians (AOH), an Irish Catholic Fraternal Organization. Kearney, an ardent Democrat, was Staten Island's public administrator (1974–1995). The AOH's JFK and St. Columcille divisions meet in West Brighton and Rossville, respectively. The St. Columcille Cultural Center, Snug Harbor and the SI Pipes and Drums maintain Irish traditions in a borough marked by the legacy of Irish Americans Monsignor Joseph A. Farrell, Father John Drumgoole, three borough presidents and Assemblywoman Elizabeth A. Connelly. The St. Patrick's Day parade (since 1964) and the annual Irish Fair (since 1998) each draw over five thousand spectators.

STATEN ISLAND HINDU TEMPLE
SEE RELIGION

BRIGHTON HEIGHTS REFORMED CHURCH

320 St. Mark's Place, St. George

Since 2006, June has been declared National Caribbean-American Heritage Month to recognize the contributions of Caribbean immigrants to this nation. By the 1930s, Staten Island was already home to a number of Caribbean immigrants, including many who worshipped at Bethel Community Church in Tompkinsville (51 Van Duzer Street). Today, this diverse community is represented at many religious, civic and culinary sites in the borough, notably at the Brighton Heights Reformed Church in St. George. Daniel Tompkins, a governor of New York and former vice president of the United States, was instrumental in founding this church in 1817. In 1864, architect John Correja designed a new structure, with a prominent spire, that was destroyed in a 1996 fire. The pastor, the Reverend James Seawood, born in Arkansas, was in Haiti during the devastating 2010 earthquake.

"A Land of Opportunity: Ven conmigo! Vieni con Me! Yee Noh!"

Aurelia Curtis, Principal, Curtis High School

Dear Friends,

The migration of people and arrival of new folk into a population are central to building societies. Theories of immigration distinguish between push and pull factors to explain the motive for emigration. These factors include better wages, natural disasters, man-made disasters (like war), poverty, better education—call it whatever you choose. I simply call it opportunity.

It was opportunity to live free of rival tribes that caused diverse tribes of Leni-Lenape Indians to settle on Staten Island over five hundred years ago. The same motivation of opportunity continued to attract others when they sought a place to call home. Each of us came to this place either because we sought opportunity or opportunity sought us. We have come from sundry places and formed communities grounded in the cultural traditions from which we came. We came with our individual and collective quests but quickly found common ground when we understood that opportunity runs true and steady, regardless of origin.

It was the opportunity of higher education that brought me to the United States and eventually to Staten Island; and what keeps me here is the ever-present opportunity to continue to improve my lot as I help to create new opportunities for others. It is Staten Island that my children call home; Staten Island that taught me the blessings of diversity and the fortitude to stand in the face of adversity; and Staten Island that offered me the opportunity to embrace a career path with tremendous promise to positively impact the very society that gave entry to global connections that enrich the world in which we live.

So, I join with many others in celebrating 350 years of opportunities that this great land has given us. Indeed, Staten Island is what we make of it. In French, we say, "*Viens avec moi*"; in Spanish, "*Ven conmigo*"; in Italian, "*Vieni con me*"; in my mother's native tongue, Bassa, "*Yee noh*"; and in English, "Come with me!" on a journey of participation and reflection on the rich history of the land that we chose because of the opportunity that it promised us—an opportunity that we continue to enjoy today!

Chapter 5

FOOD AND DRINK

si350 Inc. Committee

Contributors: Sarah Clark, Maxine Friedman, Carlotta DeFillo and Felicity Beil

"Oysters!" said Mr. Hunter. "That's how it began."

Those words, from John Mitchell's 1955 essay in the *New Yorker* entitled "Mr. Hunter's Grave," referred to the establishment of the Staten Island community known as Sandy Ground. But the statement serves well as an introduction to the history of food and drink on Staten Island. The oystering traditions of the Lenape were adapted by the first settlers of New Netherland. As Staten Island's population and economy grew, local oysters became increasingly renowned. By the late nineteenth century, people dining in New York City's oyster bars or as far away as London enjoyed oysters from Staten Island.

Over the past two centuries, Irish stew and soda bread, bratwurst and fresh pasta and pizza have been prominent on Staten Island tables. Some local establishments use wood-fired brick ovens to make pizza, but brick ovens have a history that goes back to colonial times. They were essential kitchen equipment in houses like those at Historic Richmond Town, where fresh-baked pies and breads are still prepared. In any time period, the aromas and flavors of home cooking evoke the hospitality of family and friends gathered for a meal.

Public eateries and shops also contribute to the island's individual and collective histories. These places provide common ground where neighbors meet, friendships are formed, romances blossom and milestones are celebrated. Their offerings have continually evolved with the growing diversity of the population. "Once upon a time, a large portion of veal

Sandy Ground oystermen tonging in the Arthur Kill. Local African Americans were a vital part of Staten Island's dominant shellfishing industry from the 1830s to the 1920s. *Courtesy of the Staten Island Museum.*

parmigiana with sauced up pasta served with a potato croquette made a remarkably unique meal," said Pamela Silvestri, *Staten Island Advance* food editor and restaurant critic. "Now we see an amazing inventory of ethnic restaurants and well-stocked, family-run grocery stores that are a boon for the adventurous home cook: ingredients for subcontinent, Asian and Middle Eastern meals are accessible and increasingly popular."

Over time, menus have broadened, but the essential role of food and drink in Staten Island's history and culture remains constant.

Little Sri Lanka

New Asha Restaurant, 322 Victory Boulevard, Tompkinsville
Dosa Garden, 323 Victory Boulevard, Tompkinsville
San Rasa Gourmet Restaurant, 226 Bay Street, Tompkinsville

Richly seasoned black curry, coconut sambol and *masala dosa* are among the dishes that have made Staten Island a world-class destination for lovers of authentic Sri Lankan food. Specialty stores and restaurants like New Asha and Dosa Garden are the indicators of the thriving Sri Lankan community—five thousand strong, comprising one-third of those living in New York City—present on Staten Island. In 1995, Lakruwana Wijesinghe opened in Manhattan one of the first Sri Lankan restaurants in the United States. After it closed in 2003, he moved the gourmet offerings to San Rasa.

WEST AFRICAN DELIGHTS

Mai Africa, 74 Victory Boulevard, Tompkinsville
African Homeland Store, 70 Victory Boulevard, Tompkinsville

Dishes like *fufu* and *dumboy* were introduced to the local cuisine when Esther Brown created Korto's Place, a catering business in Stapleton that lasted from 1999 to 2010. Brown, a refugee from Liberia, found assistance from the New York Association for New Americans (NYANA), a nonprofit organization initially formed to help Jewish refugees after World War II. Since then, other West African shops and eateries have prospered, including the Nigerian-owned African Homeland Store. Mia Diop's Mai Africa serves Senegalese- and French-flavored dishes, such as lamb in peanut stew, tilapia and thiakry, a pudding made with couscous, yogurt and sour cream. An outdoor West African food stand can also be found in Clifton on Sobel Court.

PROJECT HOSPITALITY

514 Bay Street, Stapleton

Project Hospitality Food and Nutrition Services provides one million meals annually through soup kitchen and food pantry services. Since its 1982 founding, Project Hospitality has spread the message "Share your bread with the hungry, and bring the homeless poor into your house" (Isaiah 58:7) and expanded to provide shelter, clothing and a broad array of care and outreach services.

RUBSAM & HORRMANN'S ATLANTIC BREWERY
SEE BUSINESS AND THE ECONOMY

THE CUP

388 Van Duzer Street, Stapleton (Former Site)

The Cup offered a venue for local artists, musicians and writers. It opened in August 2001 as the Muddy Cup, under original owner Joe Carabetta.

Historical details of the building's interior, such as tin ceilings and crown moldings, added to the eclectic atmosphere, but financial challenges caused it to close in August 2010.

DEMYAN'S HOFBRAU

730 Van Duzer Street, Stapleton (Former Site)

Years before it was Demyan's, the site was occupied by Bechtel's Brewery, the largest brewery on Staten Island in the 1880s. Bechtel's operated there for seventy-eight years and was carved into the serpentine hillside to form caves for storing beer. Frank J. Demyan Sr. and his wife, Ann, opened Demyan's Hofbrau in the 1960s as a German American restaurant and bar, later expanding operations into the caves created by the brewery. After a fire closed Demyan's, the site was occupied by a dance club. Demyan's is best remembered for displaying work by local artists, including John Noble, for its connection to fraternities at Wagner College and for providing catering to the crew of *The Godfather* during filming on Staten Island.

For over twenty-five years, Felix Imperial and his staff have provided Filipino foods on Staten Island. *Courtesy of Willie Chu, 2008.*

PHIL-AM FOODS

527 Tompkins Avenue, Rosebank

For over twenty-five years, Phil-Am Foods has served Staten Island as a grocery store specializing in Filipino products, such as *Sinigang* soup, *pancit canton* (stir-fried noodles), *Menudo* (stew) and fresh desserts. Founded in Travis in 1985, the store moved four years later to its current location. Other local groups also serve the estimated twelve thousand Filipinos residing in the borough in 2010. Since 1978, the Philippine-American Civic & Cultural Community of Staten Island (PACCCSI) has promoted Filipino American heritage through a united spirit of "bayanihan." The local San Lorenzo Ruiz Association maintains many religious traditions, notably the *Simbang Bagi*, or nine masses before Christmas, some of which are said locally in Tagalog, the native language of the Philippines.

BASILIO INN

6 Galesville Court, Arrochar

Celebrating its ninetieth year, Basilio Inn is the oldest restaurant still operating on Staten Island. Basilio Giovannini, a cooper from Piedmont, Italy, established the inn in 1921. Basilio Inn re-creates the atmosphere of the countryside of Piedmont with a grape arbor and vegetable garden used for cooking, as well as a bocce court. Social activities such as winemaking made it a center of New York's Italian community in its early days. In the 1970s, Giovanni Asperti of Naples and his family took over, and they have kept it true to its origins in appearance and menu offerings.

BOCELLI RESTAURANT

1250 Hylan Boulevard, Old Town

A more recent generation of Italian immigrants, co-owners Maria Buonsante, Vincent DeMonte and Stefano Sena (executive chef), came to New York in the 1960s. They have created a four-star restaurant that was ranked no. 1 in Zagat's 2009 Staten Island survey.

COLONNADE DINER

2001 Hylan Boulevard, Grant City

As part of the "city that never sleeps," Staten Islanders are accustomed to being able to get a bite to eat at any hour of the day or night. The Colonnade Diner, established in 1976 by the Platis family, is one of many twenty-four-hour Greek-owned diners that have served Staten Islanders since the early 1900s. Today, there are over a dozen Greek-run food establishments on the island, including Andrew's Diner, 4160 Hylan Boulevard, Eltingville, and Mike's Place, 4677 Hylan Boulevard, Annadale.

Q SINY Restaurant

632 Midland Avenue, Midland Beach (Former Site)

Gay and lesbian bars on Staten Island go back to the late 1950s, when gay men socialized at the Mayfair Bar in St. George in the evenings. Beginning in the 1970s, Sandcastle in South Beach and Beachhaven in Rosebank opened. Jamaican-born poet Michelle Cliff immortalized the Staten Island lesbian bar in her fictional short story "Rubicon." Lambda Associates of Staten Island organized annual dances in the 1980s. On July 18, 2009, the Q SINY club became Staten Island's most recent LGBT nightclub, but it closed in October 2010. The building façade, which includes the sign for the old Lincoln Hotel, has been carefully preserved.

Tavern on the Green

2566 Hylan Boulevard, New Dorp (Former Site)

Publicized in the 1960s as "Staten Island's Foremost Restaurant," Tavern on the Green welcomed Presidents Nixon and Johnson, Yogi Berra and actress Myrna Loy. It opened in 1938 in the building that originally housed the Tysen Manor Golf Club and was once part of the Guyon-Lake-Tysen farm. A later owner constructed a five-hundred-seat addition to the restaurant, which was a landmark until its closing in 1976. It is still fondly recalled by many.

Sedutto's Ice Cream

314 New Dorp Lane, New Dorp

Staten Island ice cream parlors have been providing scoops of happiness for many years. Stechmann's Ice Cream Parlor in Port Richmond was a favorite meeting place for teenagers from 1936 to 1975. The Sedutto's brand was manufactured in a factory on Richmond Terrace in Port Richmond.

Its Staten Island's Own line, created in 1994, was sold in special cartons that listed Staten Island town names. Although the Port Richmond plant closed in 1995, the Sedutto's brand still thrives, especially on New Dorp Lane, where the Sedutto's ice cream parlor has stood for about sixty years.

TASTE OF INDIA II

287 New Dorp Lane, New Dorp

Taste of India II, Staten Island's first Indian restaurant, uses ingredients and traditional recipes from the diversity of India's climates. Raman Kumar of New Delhi opened the restaurant here in 1989, two decades after his arrival. The menu, which includes a weekend buffet, satisfies vegetarians, vegans and omnivores.

NETCOST MARKET

3155 Amboy Road, Oakwood Heights

This market specializes in Russian and Eastern European food, with a wide choice of cheeses, sausages, fish and chocolates. Some products, such as herring, delicatessen and bread, are prepared by NetCost, which aims to be the "Costco of Eastern European food." Originally founded by Russian Jewish immigrant Sam Shnayder, NetCost Markets currently operates six stores. Recent census estimates indicate that over twenty-two thousand Staten Island residents came here from Russia, Ukraine and other lands of the former Soviet Union.

HOLTERMANN'S BAKERY

405 Arthur Kill Road, Great Kills

For well over a century, Holtermann's Bakery has provided fresh-baked goods that reflect German baking traditions. The business was founded in 1878 by Claus Holtermann, a German immigrant. His first bakery was located in a circa 1700 building that is now known as Historic Richmond Town's Treasure House. In 1930, the family moved the bakery to its present location.

HISTORIC RICHMOND TOWN'S GUYON-LAKE-TYSEN HOUSE

Richmond Road at Arthur Kill Road, Richmond

Historic Richmond Town staff prepare apple pie and *kool slau* (Dutch cabbage salad) in the kitchen of the Guyon-Lake-Tysen House in 2008. *Courtesy of Jeffrey D.G. Cavorley, Staten Island Historical Society.*

At Historic Richmond Town, the kitchen of the Guyon-Lake-Tysen House is still used today to demonstrate early American cooking and baking techniques. The kitchen, a circa 1820 addition to the house, was used by Mary Gifford Lake. Many of her ingredients undoubtedly came from the family's 112-acre farm, which, like many island farms, grew Indian corn, wheat and other grains and vegetables that they marketed to Manhattan and Brooklyn. Cows, sheep, hogs and chickens were also common on island farms. Visitors to Historic Richmond Town can also tour the general store across the street, managed by Sarah Black and her sisters in the 1800s, or enjoy a tradition of hospitality at the winter Tavern Concert series.

HISTORIC RICHMOND TOWN'S DECKER FARM

435 Richmond Hill Road, New Springville

These eleven acres have been farmed for more than two centuries, and the farmhouse dates to circa 1810. Japhet and Sarah Decker Alston built the house for their growing family, which eventually included twelve children. In 1841, the Alstons sold the house and property to Lorenzo Decker, and members of the Decker family retained ownership until 1955. Soil that once supported crops like wheat, corn and cabbage now nurtures tomatillos, pumpkins and other fresh produce on sale each weekend. The diminutive size of the house and the spring eave forming the front porch are typical of Staten Island's early houses, as are the Greek Revival porch posts. While virtually every other farm in New York City has been lost to development, a conservation and preservation easement ensures that Historic Richmond Town will maintain an agricultural oasis here for generations to come.

Once located at the Coney Island train yard in Brooklyn, this subway car was brought by Marvin Golden and Ray Schwartz to Golden's Kosher Deli and Restaurant for its 1981 opening. *Courtesy of Steve White.*

GOLDEN'S KOSHER DELI AND RESTAURANT

2845 Richmond Avenue, New Springville

Many kosher restaurants and food stores have been established over the years to serve the island's Jewish residents. A notable example is Golden's Kosher Deli and Restaurant, which for thirty years has offered a wide variety of traditional Jewish foods. A unique feature of Golden's is the subway car that serves as the restaurant's centerpiece.

AL DEPPE'S

Richmond Avenue and Arthur Kill Road, Greenridge (Former Site)

In the mid-twentieth century, Al Deppe's sign proudly proclaimed "Food and Fun since '21." The business began by selling balloons and expanded by moving a

"Famous Home Made Frankfurters" were prominently featured at Al Deppe's Restaurant, Greenridge, in 1952. *Photograph by Herbert A. Flamm. Courtesy of Staten Island Historical Society.*

remodeled chicken coop to the site for cooking and selling hot dogs, served on rolls from nearby Holtermann's Bakery. In the 1920s, the business had no running water or electricity, but kerosene, ingenuity and visits to O'Leary's Ice House kept the food coming and customers happy. When Al Deppe's closed in 1966, it had an expanded menu and "fun" like pinball machines and carnival games, such as skeeball.

CARMEN'S RESTAURANT

750 Barclay Avenue, Annadale

For more than fifty years, Carmen's has been serving up delicious paellas and other Spanish and American specialties. Situated on the waterfront, it is located next to the former site of Spanish Camp, founded in 1929 by anarchists from Spain. Spanish Camp's most famous resident was Dorothy Day (1897–1980), who founded the Catholic Worker movement. Although Spanish Camp no longer exists, Carmen's Restaurant thrives, thanks to good food and a great ocean view.

THE SEGUINE MANSION (FORMER SITE OF OYSTERING)

SEE ARCHITECTURE

THE CRACKER BARREL

180 Main Street, Tottenville

This building has always had a connection to food and drink. Built around 1870 as the Pepper and Joline General Store, its large second-floor hall was used by many community groups. In the 1930s, its central location in the prosperous town of Tottenville made it a perfect site for a Roulston grocery store, part of a chain with fifty stores on Staten Island at that time. By the 1960s, this location became the Cracker Barrel, a local corner store still in operation today.

Killmeyer's Old Bavaria Inn

4254 Arthur Kill Road, Charleston

In 1859, German immigrant Nicholas Killmeyer opened his inn in the town of Kreischerville (today known as Charleston) to serve local German factory workers. Still operating at the same location, Killmeyer's may be the oldest tavern on Staten Island. In 1959, owner "Cap" Simonson renamed it Century Inn to honor its one-hundred-year anniversary. In 1995, its current owners, Ken and Elise Tirado, changed the name to Killmeyer's Old Bavaria Inn to restore its German history and heritage.

Supreme Chocolatier
(Formerly Superior Confections)

1150 South Avenue, Bloomfield

This family business began in 1911, when Emmanuel Katsoris, an immigrant from Molaous, Greece, opened a candy and ice cream store in Port Richmond. Following in his footsteps, his sons, Peter and George, also manufactured chocolates, and over the years, they operated plants in Stapleton, Richmond and Travis. Their chocolates were produced under their own company name, Superior Confections, as well as for other familiar brands, including Russell Stover, Fanny Farmer and Whitman's. Today, Superior Confections are produced by the third generation of the Katsoris family, under the name Supreme Chocolatier.

Weissglass Gold Seal Dairy Corporation

2014 Forest Avenue, Mariners Harbor (Former Site)

Dairy farming and the processing and packaging of milk products were once important local activities, embodied by the Weissglass Gold Seal Dairy Corporation (formerly Weissglass Dairies, Inc.). Julius Weissglass, a Jewish immigrant from Austria, founded the company in 1899, locating it on a farm on Watchogue Road. In 1933, the firm opened a large milk processing and

This milk delivery wagon, circa 1910, was used by Weissglass Gold Seal Dairy Corporation in parades. *Courtesy of Staten Island Historical Society.*

bottling plant in Mariners Harbor. The plant remained in operation until 1975, when the business moved to Jamaica, Queens.

Mecca Mart

2111 Forest Avenue, Mariners Harbor

Omar Shakour, a Palestinian and former engineer, opened this Middle Eastern supermarket to share his culture. "There is a growing population of Arabs on Staten Island," he said, "but we also wanted to introduce our food to Americans. This store is not only for Arabs; we have customers from the Balkans, Turkey and other Mediterranean countries, including Italy—it's multicultural." Among its products are pickled wild cucumbers from Lebanon, spicy preserved lemons from Egypt, finely ground cracked wheat from Turkey, couscous from Morocco, classic pastries from Syria, dates from Jordan and Saudi Arabia and halal meat.

Ralph's Famous Italian Ices

501 Port Richmond Avenue, Port Richmond

In 1928, Italian immigrant Ralph Silvestro began selling ices from a truck; then, he opened his store here in 1945. Ralph's family oversaw the expansion of the business throughout the New York metro area. This location, the original Ralph's site, has become an essential summertime meeting place for both neighbors and "food tourists." Water ice and cream ice, in a range of traditional and exotic flavors, are the specialties of the house.

DENINO'S PIZZERIA TAVERN

524 Port Richmond Avenue, Port Richmond

John and Mary Denino established their tavern in 1937, and their son, Carlo, is credited with introducing pizza to the menu. His signature pies influenced recipes throughout the region, via family and friends who learned at his side and went on to open restaurants of their own. A street sign was dedicated in his honor in 2003, declaring Hooker Place at Port Richmond Avenue to be "Carlo Denino's Way." Many Staten Islanders are loyal to pizza made near their own homes, but Denino's is a true New York City landmark, appreciated far beyond the neighborhood.

MEZCAL'S RESTAURANT

20 Bradley Avenue, Meiers Corners

Mezcal's opened at this site in 2006, and it is a fine example of the family-owned restaurants that have introduced Staten Islanders to the cuisines and entertainment of diverse cultures. Moises Gallardo, founder of Mezcal's, came to New York from Puebla, Mexico, and opened his first restaurant in Brooklyn in 1989. Authentic meals and colorful décor offer a taste of the Mexican heritage shared by many Staten Islanders. Staten Island's Mexican-born population began growing dramatically in the 1990s.

ALFONSO PASTRY SHOPPE

1899 Victory Boulevard, Castleton Corners

Alfonso is one of many Staten Island bakeries that specialize in Italian recipes, each neighborhood having its own favorite. Alfonso is well known for cannolis, cookies and other desserts at this and two other locations.

MORE TASTES OF STATEN ISLAND

Residents and visitors can enjoy foods from the ethnic to the gourmet at additional sites listed below and at annual events, such as Historic Richmond Town's "Uncorked" each May, at the Polish and Pakistani festivals at Snug Harbor every summer and at the Greek Festival at Holy Trinity–St. Nicholas Church each September.

Vietnamese: Staten Island's first Vietnamese restaurant, Pho Mac, 1407 Richmond Avenue, Graniteville, was opened in 2005 by Andy and Kenneth Mac of Hai Phong, Vietnam.

Thai: Talay Thai, 1491 Hylan Boulevard, Dongan Hills.

Japanese/Sushi: Fushimi, 2110 Richmond Road, Grant City.

Continental: Carol's Café, 1571 Richmond Road, Dongan Hills, ranked first in Zagat's 2011 Staten Island survey.

German: For over seventy-five years, Bill "Winky" Schaffer and family have been the owners of Schaffer's, 2055 Victory Boulevard, Meiers Corners. Seasonal German beer on tap complements the authentic fare there and at Nurnberer Bierhaus, 877 Castleton, West Brighton.

Russian: Smoked fish, Ukranian borscht, chicken *tabaka* and duck are favorites at Island Grill, 4029 Hylan Boulevard, Great Kills.

Polish: The Polish Place, 19 Corson Avenue, Tompkinsville, a restaurant and market, offers homemade pierogis, Chrobry (pot roast) and much more.

Italian: Among the newer offerings, Entoca Maria, 27 Hyatt Street, St. George, and Trattoria Romano, 1476 Hylan Boulevard, Old Town, stand out. John and Joe Toto's, 809 Father Capodanno Boulevard, Ocean Breeze, and Nunzio's, 2155 Hylan Boulevard, Grant City, are neighborhood favorites.

Greek: Mike's Place, 4677 Hylan Boulevard, Annadale.

Barbecue: Wild Boar Inn, 507 Seguine Avenue, Prince's Bay.

Cajun-Creole: Bayou, 1072 Bay Street, Rosebank.

Southwestern: Enjoy beer from 130 countries and Tex-Mex fare at Adobe Blues, 63 Lafayette Avenue, New Brighton.

Mexican: Monte Alban Supermarket, 170 Port Richmond Avenue (Bennett Street), Port Richmond.

On the Beach: South Fin Grill, 300 Father Capodanno Boulevard, South Beach.

Ice Cream: Egger's Ice Cream Parlor, 1194 Forest Avenue, West Brighton.

PASTOSA RAVIOLI

764 Forest Avenue, West New Brighton

Approximately one-third of Staten Islanders today identify themselves as Italian American, so it's not surprising that Pastosa Ravioli expanded from its Brooklyn stores by adding one on Staten Island. The original business began in 1967 as the dream of Anthony G. Ajello, a cheese salesman who wanted to supply quality ravioli to customers. Today, it has grown to eleven stores throughout the New York City region, with three Staten Island locations managed by grandson Vincent D'Antunono. Ravioli and mozzarella are still made in the store today.

JODY'S CLUB FOREST

372 Forest Avenue, West New Brighton

Jody's Club Forest, which Joseph F. "Jody" Haggerty opened in 1968, represents a well-known American phenomenon: the neighborhood bar as a center of the community. Jody's is home to an annual breakfast hosted by the local city council representative in honor of the grand marshal of Staten Island's Saint Patrick's Day parade, the second-largest St. Patrick's Day Parade in the nation after Manhattan. Jody's sits in an ethnically mixed community with Irish roots. Nearby is the Wild Goose, a neighborhood bar that hosts Irish music "sessions" that follow Irish performance traditions and arrangements.

Chapter 6

THE ARTS

Meg Ventrudo

Contributors: Mary L. Bullock,
Christopher Mulé and Jim Coffey

From the waterfront of the Arthur Kill to the streets of *Shaolin*, Staten Island has long provided inspiration for writers, musicians, poets, photographers and artists.

The artists, writers, musicians, actors and photographers who once called Staten Island home are as varied as the art forms they created. Artist Jasper Cropsey, of the Hudson River School, captured Staten Island's magnificent landscape in his mid-nineteenth-century paintings. *New York Tribune* drama critic William Winter, friend of Walt Whitman, entertained in his New Brighton home Shakespearean actor Edwin Booth and writer Henry Wadsworth Longfellow. Photographer Alice Austen, at the turn of the twentieth century, and painter John Noble, two generations later, were both inspired by the waterfront. Harlem renaissance poet Langston Hughes worked one summer on the Criaris farm in Bulls Head, while feminist poet Audre Lorde wrote of flying over the Verrazano bridge. One of six local Pulitzer Prize winners, Paul Zindel earned acclaim for his play capturing suburban teenage angst. And actors Paul Newman and Martin Sheen (born Ramon Estevez), Kiss rock star Gene Simmons and folksinger Joan Baez lived here in their youth.

The venues that house the arts included regal art deco movie houses, such as the Paramount, the Ritz, the Lane and the St. George Theatre. Once home to dozens of vaudeville theaters, Staten Island hosted *Buffalo Bill's Wild West* and early film studios, featuring stars like native-born Mabel Normand. More recently, the island served as locations for films like *Working Girl*, *The Godfather*, *School of Rock*, *Easy Money* and *War of the Worlds*; television hits such as *Law and Order* and *Education of Max Bickford*; and music videos, most famously Madonna's *Papa Don't Preach*.

Today, Staten Island is home to eleven museums and historic sites with six attractions located on the grounds of the Snug Harbor Cultural Center and Botanical Garden. Since 2006, the Staten Island Film Festival has hosted independent and international films. Many living musicians still call the island their home, including David Johansen, lead singer for the New York Dolls; Vernon Reid, lead guitarist from the band Living Colour; Galt MacDermot, author of the musical *Hair*; and some members of the Wu-Tang Clan. Grass-roots organizations like Second Saturday and Art by the Ferry continue to provide showcases for a thriving community of local artists.

JASPER CROPSEY AT THE STATEN ISLAND MUSEUM

75 Stuyvesant Place, St. George

Jasper Francis Cropsey (1823–1900) was a first-generation landscape artist of the Hudson River School, and his *Looking Oceanward from Todt Hill* (1895) is a notable part of the Staten Island Museum's collection. Born on Staten Island, he suffered from periods of poor health and taught himself to draw while convalescing at his family's farm in Rossville. Cropsey began his professional career as an architect, and he designed the Moravian Church in New Dorp. His eye for meticulous detail was well suited for landscapes, and his work soon earned him entry into the National Academy of Design, becoming its youngest member at twenty-one. He and wife Maria lived in Europe for seven years. The English so appreciated Cropsey's use of vibrant colors that he was referred to as "America's Painter of Autumn." He purchased a home and studio he called Ever Rest at Hastings-on-Hudson, New York, in 1885 and remained there until his death in 1900. An important early landscape painting by Cropsey, *Cortelyou Farm Greenridge*, is in the SIHS collection, Historic Richmond Town.

McKEE TECHNICAL AND VOCATIONAL HIGH SCHOOL

290 St. Marks Place, New Brighton

Though not typically associated with the arts, McKee High School employed Frank McCourt (1930–2009) as an English teacher for several years, starting in 1958. McCourt went on to teach creative writing at Stuyvesant High School and achieved international acclaim with the 1996 publication of *Angela's Ashes*, a gripping account of the deep poverty his family experienced in Brooklyn and Ireland. McCourt received the Pulitzer Prize and the National Book Critics Circle Award for this memoir. His other notable works include *'Tis* and *Teacher Man*, which describes the challenges of being a young, uncertain teacher.

St. George Theatre

35 Hyatt Street, St. George

When the St. George Theatre opened on December 4, 1929, the island's newest movie and vaudeville house outshone most of its competitors of the day, including Manhattan's Capitol Theatre on Broadway. The interior contains features in the Spanish and Italian Baroque styles. Large stained-glass chandeliers illuminate the foyer, majestic staircases lead up to an elaborate mezzanine level and murals, tiled fountains and sculpted figures set in niches adorn much of the building. The theater fell on hard times in the 1970s and was closed for over three decades. In 2004, three women prevented its demolition, and today, the newly renovated St. George Theatre is run by a nonprofit organization and serves as a cultural and performing arts center for myriad activities.

The St. George Theatre, located only steps from the Staten Island Ferry, has been restored as a major cultural and performing arts center for Staten Island and all of New York City. *Courtesy of Staten Island Advance.*

"A DREAM: SAVE THE ST. GEORGE THEATRE"

Doreen Cugno, Executive Director, Saint George Theatre

Dear Friends,

It's with great pride that we say, happy birthday to Staten Island!

My mother's dream of saving the majestic St. George Theatre may have originated during her childhood years. According to my grandmother, Rose McKee, my mother loved to "create" a theater in her family's Midland Beach home for all the neighborhood children to enjoy. In those days, many families didn't own a television set. Her family was the first on the block to sport this new invention.

With kitchen chairs strategically placed in the family's living room, a young Mrs. Rosemary strolled down the center "aisle," brandishing a flashlight. Grandma Rose, a teacher at St. Margaret Mary's School, had to remind my mother not to bop her guests on the head with the flashlight; but, as mom explained, she simply wanted order in her "theatre." Guests (aka her brothers and friends) were then treated to a preshow performance by my grandfather, Irving McKee, playing the banjo, while my mother tap danced.

Later, as a young teen, my mother often visited the theater with her siblings to watch the double feature films. Then as an adult, my mother rented the St. George Theatre in the 1950s, '60s and '70s to host the Mrs. Rosemary annual dance recitals. My sisters and I have fond memories of performing there during our childhood years as young dancers in our mother's dance school, located first in South Beach and, since 1972, in New Dorp.

In 2004, my mother, along with my sister Luanne and I, saved the St. George Theatre from being torn down. With my mom's life savings donated, and the support from the Staten Island community, we began to renovate and develop a performing arts center for Staten Islanders and all New Yorkers to enjoy. Who knew my mother's dreams of being a theater matron would see their way to fruition with this incredible and ambitious endeavor!

All one needs to do is walk inside this historic theater to feel the presence of Mrs. Rosemary's passion for the arts. In that spirit, my sisters and I are proud and honored to continue carrying on our mother's dream. These days, however, flashlights are only used for lighting the aisles.

On behalf of my sisters Luanne and Rosemary, we want to thank all Staten Islanders for supporting the arts and especially the St. George Theatre. Happy Birthday, Staten Island, and many more!

North Shore Arts Venues

St. George

Everything Goes Book Café and Neighborhood Stage (208 Bay Street) provides its community with a place to meet, exchange ideas, see art and listen to music and stories performed on stage. Visible from the ferry terminal, SHOW Gallery, Studio and Performance Space (156 Stuyvesant Place) hosts installations direct from larger venues, such as the World Financial Center, and puts on exhibitions, performances and workshops by local and internationally known artists. Galerie St. George (11 Phelps Place) is an international art gallery with works on paper, paintings, sculpture, fabric collage, furniture and photographs.

Century Dance Complex

568 Bay Street, Stapleton

A native of Liberia, Rose Kingston founded Century Dance Complex (CDC) in 2006. At age nine, she lived in a refugee camp in Ghana before her family was granted asylum to the United States. Through war, displacement, poverty and family separation, Kingston found a therapeutic outlet in dance. CDC's mission is to provide a safe haven for refugees and underprivileged children to learn, explore and reach their highest potential through arts, educational and job readiness programs and community outreach. The CDC hosts an annual cultural event in Tappen Park to celebrate diversity through the arts and enable youth to share the stage with accomplished artists.

The Century Dance Complex Kids-n-Teens perform at the Fifth Annual Staten Island International Dance Festival at Tappen Park in August 2010. *Courtesy of Christopher Mulé.*

AUDRE LORDE HOME

207 St. Paul's Avenue, Stapleton

"Leaving, leaving the bridged water beneath the red sands of South Beach" begins the poem "On My Way Out I Passed Over You and the Verrazano Bridge," by Audre Lorde (1934–1992). Lorde lived in Stapleton from 1972 to 1987. Calling herself a "black feminist lesbian mother poet," because her identity was based on the relationship of many divergent perspectives once perceived as incompatible, Lorde was a prolific writer. In 1975, she was named Woman of the Year by Staten Island Community College, where LGBT and other civic-minded academics thrived. In 1979, Lorde spoke before seventy-five thousand people at the First National March for Gay and Lesbian Liberation in Washington, D.C.

PARK HILL APARTMENTS

Vanderbilt and Park Hill Avenues, Clifton

Staten Island's Wu-Tang Clan became arguably the most influential rap group of the mid-1990s. A loosely based organization of nine rappers— U-God, RZA, Raekwon, Ol Dirty Bastard, Method Man, Masta Killa, Inspectah Deck, GZA/Genius and Ghostface—the collective recorded together and released albums as solo artists. Most of its members grew up in the publicly subsidized Park Hill Apartments and drew material from that experience for their sound scapes and raps. The group created a clothing store at 61 Victory Boulevard in Tompkinsville, now a barbershop, Against Da Grain.

ALICE AUSTEN HOUSE

2 Hylan Boulevard, Rosebank

This picturesque Gothic Revival cottage overlooking the Narrows began as a late seventeenth-century farmhouse and was enhanced by John Austen, a prosperous New York City merchant, with the addition of a vine-covered veranda and peaked dormers in carpenter Gothic style. In infancy,

Alice Austen, one of the earliest celebrated American female photographers, captured this image of the Ward family. Violet Ward authored a book on *Bicycling for Young Ladies* (1896), which featured Austen's photos. *Photograph by Alice Austen. Courtesy of Staten Island Historical Society.*

granddaughter Alice Austen (1866–1952) moved here with her mother. At the age of eleven, her Uncle Oswald, a Danish sea captain, brought back a dry plate camera from one of his voyages. Her Uncle Peter, a chemistry professor at Rutgers University, taught Austen how to use the chemicals to develop photographs. A dark room was installed in an upstairs storage closet at their home, also known as Clear Comfort. Austen spent many years carrying around almost fifty pounds of equipment, photographing all aspects of city life, including boot blacks, the waterfront, family, friends and athletic events. The Staten Island Historical Society collection contains more than seven thousand of Austen's original photographic prints and negatives.

FRED SCOTT MOVIE RANCH/SOUTH BEACH ARCADE

Sand Lane and Father Capodanno Boulevard, South Beach (Former Site)

Staten Islanders Fred Scott and Mabel Normand (1892–1930) played significant roles in the birth of the American motion picture industry at the start of the twentieth century. Scott constructed the Movie Ranch on his

South Beach farm, complete with Western "sets" to accommodate studios seeking interesting locations to film. The 1914 serial *The Perils of Pauline* is arguably the most recognizable of the many silent movies filmed here. Born in New Brighton, comedic actress Normand is credited with creating the famous "pie in the face" gag. The South Beach Arcade, 300 Sand Lane, a favorite of local children through the 1990s, marked the location where the Movie Ranch once stood.

LANE THEATER

168 New Dorp Lane, New Dorp

The last pre–World War II movie house built on Staten Island, the Lane Theater opened on February 10, 1938, as part of an architectural plan that included the five storefronts adjacent to the theater entrance. Designed by preeminent theater architect John Eberson, it featured a futuristically styled celestial ceiling and was the first theater to display fluorescent murals lit in black light. The inside of this 588-seat, single-screen venue is one of the last remaining examples of the art moderne/art deco style of theaters in New York City, and the Lane was designated a New York City Interior Landmark in 1988.

JACQUES MARCHAIS MUSEUM OF TIBETAN ART

SEE ARCHITECTURE

WILLIAM PAGE AND GREGORY PERILLO HOMES

Near Southwest Corner of Hylan Boulevard and Page Avenue, Tottenville (Former Site) Wards Point Avenue, Tottenville

In 1865, the internationally renowned portraitist William Page (1811–1885) built an octagonal house on eight acres in Tottenville, a town that has long attracted prominent artists. Page had studied painting under Samuel F.B.

Morse and for eleven years lived in Rome, where he painted portraits of friends, such as Robert and Elizabeth Barrett Browning. Gregory Perillo (born 1931) grew up on Staten Island, moving to Tottenville in 1984. A nationally known artist depicting Native Americans of the western frontier, Perillo combines portraits of animals and humans in a style merging realism and impressionism.

PAUL ZINDEL/TOTTENVILLE HIGH SCHOOL

100 Luten Avenue, Tottenville

Paul Zindel (1936–2003), one of six local Pulitzer Prize winners, earned that award in 1971 for one of his eight plays, *The Effect of Gamma Rays on Man-in-the-Moon Marigolds*. He also authored thirty-nine novels, including *My Darling, My Hamburger* and *The Pigman*, which are still widely read in high schools across the country. As a child, he moved frequently from place to place on Staten Island with his mother and sister after his father abandoned them, an experience that profoundly shaped his later writings. He graduated Port Richmond High School. At Wagner College, he majored in chemistry, while studying creative writing with playwright Edward Albee. He briefly worked for Allied Chemical and taught science at Tottenville High School until 1969. His "zany stories" and performances kept teenage audiences "screaming with delight."

JOSEPH PAPP GRAVE SITE

Baron Hirsch Cemetery, 1126 Richmond Avenue, Graniteville

Joseph Papp, the founder in 1951 of the New York Shakespeare Festival and the Public Theater and son of Russian-Jewish immigrants, is buried in Baron Hirsch Cemetery. He brought to the Broadway stage in 1967 *Hair* (music written by islander Galt MacDermot) and in 1975 *A Chorus Line*, one of Broadway's longest-running musicals. In 1963, Papp also gave Martin Sheen, living at 30 Daniel Lowe Terrace, Staten Island, his first important acting job.

LANGSTON HUGHES AT THE CRIARIS FARM

2289 Richmond Avenue, Bulls Head (Former Site)

Langston Hughes, who later became an acclaimed poet of the Harlem Renaissance, worked on a farm owned by Greek immigrants in Bulls Head in 1921. *Courtesy of Library of Congress.*

The summer of 1922 brought aspiring poet Langston Hughes (1902–1967) to Staten Island after he dropped out of Columbia University. In *The Big Sea* (1940), he wrote: "I finally got work at a truck-garden farm on Staten Island. The farm belonged to some Greeks [the Criaris brothers and their wives], who didn't care what nationality you were, just so you got up at five in the morning and worked all day…There was something about such work that made you feel useful and important—sending off onions that you had planted and seen grow from a mere speck of green, that you tended and weeded, had pulled up and washed and even loaded on the wagon—seeing them go off to feed the great city of New York. Your onions!" An internationally acclaimed Harlem Renaissance poet, Hughes's work continues to be celebrated at the renowned Schomburg Library in Harlem, where his ashes are interred.

ICHABOD CRANE BURIAL SITE

Asbury Methodist Cemetery, 2000 Richmond Avenue, New Springville

Colonel Ichabod Bennet Crane's (1787–1857) distinguished military career spanned forty-eight years. A chance meeting in 1814 between Crane and author Washington Irving prompted the naming of the timid and lanky fictional schoolmaster in Irving's *The Legend of Sleepy Hollow*, the antithesis of the real Crane. Moving to Staten Island in 1853, Crane lived in the Ansley farmhouse on Victory Boulevard. Upon his death, a large marble monument and spire were erected at his grave site. Neglected for years, the Asbury Cemetery Association purchased the cemetery from the City of New York in the 1990s for one dollar and restored it to its current state.

College of Staten Island
Center for the Arts/Radio Station

2800 Victory Boulevard, Willowbrook

The Center for the Arts (CFA) is one of the leading state-of-the-art performing arts centers in Staten Island. In fifteen years since its 1996 opening, the CFA has presented 310 artists and performances. The College of Staten Island also sponsors WSIA, Staten Island's only FM radio station, and counts notable artists as its graduates. Two of these include Gene Simmons and Paul Stanley. Simmons met Stanley while attending Richmond College, where he received a degree in education. After teaching for a while in Spanish Harlem, he and Stanley started KISS.

Henry David Thoreau/
The Philosopher's Retreat

Emerson Hill

In 1843, Henry David Thoreau tutored the children of Richmond County judge William Emerson, who lived in an area known as Dutch farms (now Emerson Hill). His brother, Ralph Waldo Emerson, visited there. In 1910, businessman and author Cornelius G. Kolff built a one-room log cabin on Emerson Hill, which he called the Philosopher's Retreat. Borough president George Cromwell, philanthropist and educator William G. Willcox (namesake of P.S. 48 in Grasmere) and poet Edwin Markham were among the members of the club. Markham (namesake of I.S. 51 in Willowbrook), was best known for his reading of the poem *Lincoln, Man of the People* at the dedication of the Lincoln Memorial in 1922. At each meeting, members gave a five-minute talk on a philosophical matter and then voted for the best one by secret ballot. One of the rules of the club was that women were not to be admitted; however, this rule was regularly broken by Anna (Shaw) Curtis, Carrie Chapman Catt, Ida Dudley Dale and others. The last standing log cabin in the five boroughs, the building was destroyed by fire in 1917.

DiMarzio Pickups

1388 Richmond Terrace, New Brighton

Surrounded by boatyards and houses, the DiMarzio pickup factory produces magnetic pickups for electric guitars. Lawrence DiMarzio, a guitarist and technician who was dissatisfied with the quality and sound of pickups made by the major guitar companies, began taking vintage guitar pickups apart and reconstructing them, looking to increase signal, reduce noise and create tone. He founded his business in 1975, after people began asking him to work on and eventually build them pickups. The DiMarzio factory now employs about fifty people and is known internationally for the quality of its product. Artists affiliated with the company include Al DiMeola, Joe Satriani, Steve Vai, Billy Sheehan, Rick Derringer, Earl Slick and Ace Freely.

Snug Harbor Cultural Center and Botanical Garden

See Education and Health, Architecture and Environment

Council of the Arts and Humanities of Staten Island (COAHSI)/Art Lab

1000 Richmond Terrace, Snug Harbor Cultural Center, New Brighton

A school of fine and applied art, Art Lab was established in 1975 to provide a home for quality art instruction, exhibitions and other events. The Council of the Arts and Humanities of Staten Island (COAHSI) partners on arts and humanities projects with individual artists, cultural groups, community-based organizations, businesses, schools and governmental agencies. COAHSI maintains a calendar of events and offers workshops, seminars and cultural programs.

Noble Maritime Museum

1000 Richmond Terrace, Snug Harbor Cultural Center, New Brighton

Born in Paris and a New York resident by 1919, John Noble (1913–1983) was the son of noted American painter John "Wichita Bill" Noble. From 1928 to 1945, Noble worked as a seaman on schooners and in marine salvage on the Kill van Kull. In 1941, he started to build his floating studio out of parts of salvaged vessels, and in 1946, he began working full time as an artist, documenting the industry of the harbor. Throughout his lifetime, he remained clear about his sympathies: "I am with factory people, industrial people, immigrants and sons of immigrants." His work is now housed and displayed as a separate collection at the Snug Harbor Cultural Center.

Musical Chairs Chamber Ensemble, Inc. (MCCE)

Various Venues on Staten Island

Described as "concert bliss" by the *Staten Island Advance* in 2009, Musical Chairs has entertained local audiences since 2004. Its genre-bending style, including both classical and contemporary chamber music, regularly features commissions and premieres by local and international composers. MCCE has received awards from the National Endowment for the Arts.

North Shore Community Arts Groups

St. George

The Creative Photographers' Guild formed in 2005 has a gallery at 814 Richmond Terrace. Art by the Ferry launched a June festival in 2008 to showcase local artistic talent and promote economic growth. It includes artists in all media and welcomes visitors from Staten Island and the world. Friends of Fire ceramicists staged their first holiday crafts fair in 1999. Second Saturday, a monthly art crawl, highlights the burgeoning independent art and music scene at local galleries, restaurants, stores and private homes.

MANDOLIN BROTHERS, LTD.

629 Forest Avenue, West Brighton

In business since 1971, Mandolin Brothers is one of the largest and most reputable dealers in the world of vintage and new American-fretted instruments. Known for its high level of professionalism, it has also been called a "toy store for guitar players." Mandolin Brothers has supplied instruments to well-known players and musicians, such as George Benson, Edie Brickell, Jimmy Buffett, Tom Chapin, Marc Cohn, Judy Collins, Gloria Estefan, Jay Geils, George Harrison, Janis Ian, the Indigo Girls, Chris Isaak, Lenny Kravitz, Cyndi Lauper, Lyle Lovett, Pat Matheny, Paul McCartney, Sarah McLachlan, Don McLean, John Cougar Mellencamp, Steve Miller, Joni Mitchell, Vernon Reid and Richie Sambora.

STATEN ISLAND BALLET/STATEN ISLAND SHAKESPEAREAN THEATRE/SUN DOG THEATRE

460 Brielle Avenue, Manor Heights

Located on the campus of the Sea View Farm Colony Historic District, the seventeen-year-old Staten Island Ballet annually creates four fully staged productions. Since 1975, the Staten Island Shakespearean Theatre has staged almost two hundred productions. Using venues around the island, the Actors Equity–approved Showcase Company balances works by the Bard of Avon with more contemporary shows. Sun Dog Theatre is a resident performing arts organization that emphasizes contemporary and original theater. Since 2003, Sun Dog has annually produced the well-known *Scenes from the Staten Island Ferry.*

The Staten Island Ballet is "sensuous and fierce… with a refreshing directness," according to the *New York Times. Courtesy of Amesse Photography.*

The Arts

WAGNER COLLEGE THEATER PROGRAM

1 Campus Road, Grymes Hill

Wagner College's amateur theater club, the Varsity Players, staged its first production in 1924. It was not until 1968, however, that Wagner established a formal theater major, hiring Dr. Lowell Matson to spearhead the program. By the time "Doc" retired in 1987, Wagner College had become a well-known breeding ground for Broadway talent. Since 2005, the Princeton Review has ranked the program among the top five college theaters in the country.

VIDEO ULQINI

346 Victory Boulevard, Tompkinsville

Opened in 1983 by Staten Island resident Renzi Murati and family, Video Ulqini sells cultural products from Albania to the approximately five thousand Albanians on the island. With its location across from the Albanian Islamic Cultural Center, the store caters to Muslims, but its music, movies and traditional embroidered clothing also provide a secular connection to Albania for the entire community, which includes Orthodox Christians and Catholics.

UNIVERSAL TEMPLE OF THE ARTS (UTA)

425 Jersey Street, New Brighton

Founded in 1967, UTA serves low- to moderate-income African American and Hispanic youth by offering creative services designed to develop lifelong scholars and creative thinkers. From its storefront headquarters, this grass-roots organization recruits professional artists from an eclectic blend of the fine and performing arts to teach its classes and workshops. Signature programs include quilting, sewing, visual arts, music, vocal, dance, piano, multicultural doll making, computer literacy and Jazz 4 Teens. UTA's world-class Staten Island JAZZFestival, an annual event since 1988, offers jazz lovers performances and workshops geared toward the entire family.

Chapter 7

SPORTS

Jay Price

On an overcast Wednesday afternoon in October 1951, in the bottom of the ninth inning of the third and final playoff game for the National League pennant, Bobby Thomson hit a high, inside fastball into the left field stands at the Polo Grounds for a three-run home run. The blast vaulted the New York Giants over the Brooklyn Dodgers and into the World Series, ending the most dramatic pennant race in baseball history.

In the press box, the normally unflappable radio announcer Russ Hodges stood and shouted into his microphone: "There's a long drive…it's gonna be…I believe…the Giants win the pennant! The Giants win the pennant! The Giants win the pennant!"

Everywhere there were Giants fans, grown men and women danced in the street. In Brooklyn, they cried.

Thomson dressed in the beery, chaotic euphoria of the Giants clubhouse and took a cab to midtown Manhattan, where he made a live appearance on Perry Como's weekly television show.

Then he took the ferry home to Staten Island and spent the rest of his life wondering what the fuss was all about.

Sports can inspire us or disappoint us, but at their very best, the games reflect the best in all of us. It was that way when Thomson, a cabinetmaker's son born in Scotland, hit the most famous home run in baseball history.

It was that way when Abe Kiviat, whose Polish parents still spoke Yiddish, was setting world records in the mile; when Fred "Sonny" Logan hit for the New York Black Yankees in the Negro Leagues; and when Sal Somma, a one-time high school dropout, kicked the extra point that beat Vince Lombardi and Fordham's legendary Seven Blocks of Granite. And it was that way when the Stapes, a neighborhood team playing in a wooden ballpark, played in a start-up business called the National Football League.

The athletes have gotten bigger, stronger and considerably richer. But their stories can still lift us out of our seats and make us want to cry or dance in the street. And a lot of those stories started—or were played out—on Staten Island, home of the Staten Island Scot.

RICHMOND COUNTY SAVINGS BANK BALLPARK AT ST. GEORGE

75 Richmond Terrace, St. George

Home of the Staten Island Yankees of the New York–Penn League, the 6,500-seat Richmond County Savings Bank Ballpark opened in 2001. It stands near the site of the St. George Cricket and Baseball Grounds, founded in 1872. In 1886–1887, the New York Metropolitans of the American Association and, in 1889, the Giants of the National League played here. At this site in 1874, Mary Ewing Outerbridge first introduced tennis to the United States, and the first national tennis tournament was held on September 1, 1880.

CURTIS HIGH SCHOOL

SEE EDUCATION AND HEALTH

WINTER AVENUE/LIOTTI IKEFUGI PLAYGROUND

46 Winter Avenue, New Brighton

The Winter Avenue Playground was "home court" for Elmer Ripley, a member of the National Basketball Hall of Fame. Ripley, who lived across the street from the playground, guided Georgetown to the 1943 NCAA national championship game and also coached Notre Dame, Columbia, Army, the Israeli Olympic Team and the Harlem Globetrotters. Prior to coaching, he starred with the original Celtics and the New York Nationals and was regarded as the best all-around player in the country in the early days of the sport. Originally named for theater critic William Winter, the site was renamed Liotti Ikefugi Playground in 1961 to commemorate two men killed in World War II. At age twenty, Llyod Ikefugi, born in New Brighton, became a member of the famous all Japanese American 442nd Infantry and earned a Purple Heart in Italy one year later.

CROMWELL CENTER AND LYONS POOL

Pier 6, Murray Hulbert Avenue, Tompkinsville

Cromwell Center and Lyons Pool were built during the Great Depression by the Works Progress Administration (WPA). The 1936 facility honored the first borough president, lawyer George Cromwell, who served from 1898 to 1913 and died in 1934, and World War I veteran Joseph H. Lyons. Frank Di Gennara, Staten Island's only Olympic gold-medal winner in an individual event (flyweight boxing, 1920), trained young boxers here. Cromwell Center, with its eight full basketball courts and facilities for myriad sports events, recreational activities and crafts, was a year-round destination for Staten Islanders for decades. Closed for renovations in April 2010, it collapsed into the bay a month later.

THOMPSON'S STADIUM

Tompkins Avenue at Broad Street, Stapleton (Former Site)

Thompson's Stadium occupied the current site of the Stapleton Houses. From 1929 through 1932, the National Football League's (NFL) Stapletons (also known as the Stapes) played there. The Stapes and New York Giants played here every Thanksgiving, and in one of their last league games, the Stapes held the Chicago Bears—with all-time NFL greats Red Grange and Bronco Nagurski—to a 0–0 tie. Built by the owner of a nearby lumberyard, the wooden stadium was also home to midget auto racing, barnstorming big-league baseball teams and high school football throughout the first half of the twentieth century.

ABE KIVIAT HOME

101 Broad Street, Stapleton

Abe Kiviat, a silver medal winner in the 1912 Olympic Games and a world record holder in the mile, grew up above the Stapleton store operated by his parents, Polish immigrants who still spoke Yiddish. In his brief but meteoric track career, Kiviat set fourteen individual records at distances from 600 yards to the mile, ran the anchor leg on five record-setting relay teams and once broke the world record for 1,500 meters three times in six days. As part of its centennial celebration, the Amateur Athletic Union named him the greatest indoor middle-distance runner of all time.

World record holder Abe Kiviat, third from left, ran for a silver medal in the 1,500-meter final at the 1912 Olympic Games. *Courtesy of* Staten Island Advance.

SAL SOMMA HOME

125 Greenfield Avenue, Clifton

Sal Somma, who became a legendary high school coach at New Dorp High School, grew up on what was then Simonson Avenue in a home built by the Vanderbilt family. The son of Italian immigrants and a one-time high school dropout, Somma kicked the winning point when New York University upset Vince Lombardi and Fordham's Seven Blocks of Granite to keep the Rams out of the 1937 Rose Bowl. He was the Staten Island Sports Hall of Fame's first inductee.

NEW YORK YACHT CLUB

30 Hylan Boulevard, Rosebank

The McFarlane-Bredt House, home of the New York Yacht Club from 1868 to 1871, was the site of the first defense of the America's Cup, yachting's most coveted prize and the oldest active trophy in all of international sports. As some fifty thousand spectators watched from the shores of Staten Island and Brooklyn in the summer of 1870, the American yacht *Magic* defeated sixteen other boats. *Cambria*, the English challenger, finished a distant eighth, and the race spawned yachting's most storied competition.

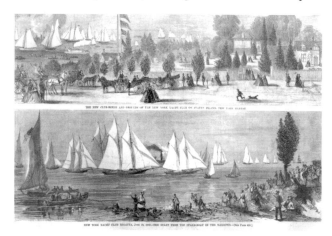

A 1868 regatta near the McFarlane-Bredt House in Rosebank, home of the New York Yacht Club, which hosted the first defense of the America's Cup (from *Harper's Weekly*). *Courtesy of Staten Island Historical Society.*

NEW YORK CITY MARATHON

Verrazano-Narrows Bridge Apron, Fort Wadsworth

Since 1976, when the route for the New York City Marathon moved from the confines of Central Park to include all five boroughs, the 26.2-mile race has started on the Staten Island side of the Verrazano-Narrows Bridge. Four-time champion Bill Rodgers won the first five-borough race, which has subsequently grown into one of the world's preeminent distance races, with most of its forty thousand annual entrants decided by lottery. Prerace activities, hosted by the National Park Service, take place on the grounds of Fort Wadsworth.

P.S. 46 Playground

Parkinson Avenue at Reid Avenue, South Beach

The P.S. 46 playground serves as the anchor of its surrounding community. Nick Fotiu, the first native New Yorker to play in the National Hockey League (NHL), initially played roller hockey on its blacktop. Fotiu, who didn't play on ice until he was a teenager, went on to establish himself as one of the NHL's toughest players, in seasons with the New York Rangers, Calgary Flames, Philadelphia Flyers, Edmonton Oilers and New England Whalers of the NHL and the Hartford Whalers of the World Hockey Association.

Hy Turkin Field

225 Seaver Avenue, Dongan Hills

Hy Turkin Field is the home field of the Staten Island Little League, the first sanctioned Little League in the borough. It opened for play in 1953 across the street on a site known as Seaver Oval. Named for the sportswriter, Hy Turkin Field was built in 1957 and, in 1961, became the first Little League field on Staten Island with lights. That same season, the league hosted the Little League East Regional, one step from the Little League World Series in Williamsport, Pennsylvania.

General Douglas MacArthur Park

202 Jefferson Street, Dongan Hills

Generations of Dongan Hills residents have come together at General Douglas MacArthur Park. Better known as the Berry Houses playground, the park has been home to the best baseball, basketball, softball and touch football leagues on Staten Island since 1951. Earlier in the century, the grounds were the site of the Richmond County Fairgrounds, which included a racing meet for standard-bred horses and, at the 1928 county fair, for greyhound racing. General MacArthur, the youngest U.S. army chief of staff in the 1930s, served in four American wars, including World War II and Korea.

SEMLER'S PARK

Lincoln and South Railroad Avenue, Grant City (Former Site)

Semler's Park, a privately owned picnic ground and ball field, was home to sandlot football teams like the Grant City Athletic Club, Staten Island Tigers and the legendary New Dorp Queens in the mid-twentieth century. Under Coach Dan Boylan, the Queens won nine championships, going undefeated five times.

BOBBY THOMSON HOME

411 Flagg Place, Dongan Hills

Bobby Thomson, Staten Island's most celebrated athlete, lived on Flagg Place in the fall of 1951, when he hit the most famous home run in baseball history. Thomson's "Shot Heard 'Round the World" lifted the New York Giants over the Brooklyn Dodgers in a 1951 National League playoff between baseball's greatest rivals. That evening, after making a live appearance on the *Perry Como Show*, the son of a Scottish cabinetmaker took the Staten Island Ferry home before starting World Series play against the Yankees the next day.

Among the most famous home runs in baseball history, Bobby Thomson's "Shot Heard 'Round the World" decided a 1951 playoff between the New York Giants and Brooklyn Dodgers. *Courtesy of* Staten Island Advance.

Richmond County Country Club

1122 Todt Hill Road, Todt Hill

The Richmond County Country Club was first organized in 1888 and moved to its present site in 1897. Its golf course, long the home of the Staten Island Amateur, boasts a 644-yard par 5, the longest in the metropolitan area. In an effort to preserve Staten Island's Greenbelt, New York state purchased the course in 1989 and awarded the club a ninety-nine-year lease at a cost of one dollar a year.

Miller Field

See Military History

Tottenville High School

100 Luten Avenue, Huguenot

Tottenville High School has produced dozens of city championship teams in a variety of sports. It is the alma mater of Joe Andruzzi and Adewale Ogunleye, two of Staten Island's most accomplished National Football League stars, and of Major League pitcher Jason Marquis. Andruzzi, an offensive guard for the New England Patriots, was an integral part of the Super Bowl championship teams of 2002, 2004 and 2005. Ogunleye, the son of Nigerian immigrants, was one of the top pass-rushers in the NFL and, in 2003, became the first Staten Islander named to the Pro Bowl.

Tottenville High School graduate Adewale Ogunleye, in action here against the New York Giants, became one of the National Football League's premier pass-rushers. *Courtesy of* Staten Island Advance.

MOUNT LORETTO, HOME OF THE STATEN ISLAND SPORTS HALL OF FAME

6581 Hylan Boulevard, Pleasant Plains

SEE ALSO EDUCATION AND HEALTH, ENVIRONMENT AND RELIGION

Mount Loretto, once the largest child-care facility in the United States, boasted a sports program that rivaled many college campuses. The Mount's Sports Nights drew some of the great sports champions of the day. In 2002, when the building that once served as the Junior Boys Gym was reborn as the Catholic Youth Organization/Mission of the Immaculate Virgin (CYO/MIV), it became the home of the Staten Island Sports Hall of Fame and museum. As of 2011, over ninety of Staten Island's greatest athletes, coaches, teams and contributors are enshrined, and their accomplishments are commemorated for all time. Among them are two-time NCAA basketball champion Nicky Anosike, ex-Mets reliever John Franco and many others.

AQUEHONGA FIELD

Amboy Road and Sprague Avenue, Tottenville (Former Site)

Once located behind the tavern of the same name, this field's name refers to the Lenape designation of Staten Island as "the Island of the dark woods on high grounds (Aquehonga Monadnock)." It was home to generations of baseball players from Staten Island's South Shore, some of whom played in their bare feet. Among the best were Glen Mosley, Julie Bowers and Fred "Sonny" Logan, who went on to play for the New York Black Yankees of the Negro Leagues. Another notable ballplayer was Herb White, an outstanding catcher in the New York Yankee organization and later the Wagner College baseball coach, who lost the best years of his baseball career serving in World War II.

MID-ISLAND LITTLE LEAGUE COMPLEX

Richmond Avenue, Graniteville (Former Site)

A twelve-year-old all-star team from the Mid-Island Little League, which played on this site before moving to a larger complex in Travis, won the

Players and coaches from Mid-Island Little League celebrate after winning the 1964 Little League World Series in Williamsport, Pennsylvania. *Courtesy of* Staten Island Advance.

1964 Little League World Series in Williamsport, Pennsylvania. In the championship game, Mid-Island's Dan Yaccarino pitched a no-hitter and hit a home run to defeat Monterey, Mexico, 4–0. These local youth won all thirteen games on their way to the championship and came home to a ticker tape parade down Broadway.

AMATEUR SOFTBALL ASSOCIATION (ASA) COMPLEX

Travis Avenue, Travis

The ASA complex has been home to top U.S. softball leagues and teams, including three-time national champion Silvestri's. It has hosted some of the nation's most competitive amateur tournaments and the Metro Bowl, between New York City's public and parochial high school softball champions. In 2000, the U.S. national team—the defending Olympic champions—played a double-header here against a team of Staten Island collegiate stars.

WEISSGLASS STADIUM

Gloria Cordes Elliott, pitcher for the Kalamazoo Lassies of the All-American Girls Professional Baseball League, was an inspiration for the movie *A League of Their Own. Courtesy of* Staten Island Advance.

Richmond Terrace at Jewett Avenue, Port Richmond (Former Site)

Weissglass Stadium, on the site previously known as Sisco Park and Braybrooks Oval, was home to most of the major sporting events on Staten Island from the 1940s to 1973. It became best known for its Saturday night stock car races and the annual Thanksgiving Day high school football game between Curtis and New Dorp High Schools, which drew crowds in excess of ten thousand. Negro League stars Satchel Paige and Josh Gibson played at Weissglass, and Gloria Cordes Elliott auditioned here on her way to the All-American Girls Professional Baseball League, memorialized in the movie *A League of Their Own.*

CYO CENTER

120 Anderson Avenue, Port Richmond

The Catholic Youth Organization's (CYO) Port Richmond center opened in 1944 and quickly became a beacon for athletes. In addition to the center's in-house leagues and after-school programs, the CYO supervises island, city and archdiocesan competitions in basketball, baseball, softball and other activities.

FAIRVIEW CEMETERY

1852 Victory Boulevard, Castleton Corners

Fairview Cemetery is the final resting place for Jack Besson Taylor, a nineteenth-century Major League pitcher who won 23, 26 and 20 games in successive seasons for the Philadelphia Phillies. The son of an oysterman who immigrated to Staten Island from Maryland, Taylor won 120 games in nine big-league seasons for the Phillies, Giants, Browns (later Cardinals) and Reds before his untimely death at age twenty-six. He was selected to the Phillies' all-time team in 1959 and is a member of the Staten Island Hall of Fame. In 2003, the Fairview board of directors dedicated a new baseball-themed headstone at Taylor's grave site.

CLOVE LAKES PARK

1150 Clove Road, West New Brighton

SEE ALSO ENVIRONMENT AND MILITARY HISTORY

Clove Lakes Park has provided public facilities—most notably baseball fields, riding trails and a skating rink—for recreational and competitive sports since the 1930s. The park hosts every major high school cross-country meet and the Lou Marli Run, Staten Island's oldest sports tradition, held on Thanksgiving Day since 1949. In 1978, the Forest Avenue park entrance became the start and finishing area for the July Fourth Pepper Martin/Arielle Newman Run, the island's first major race during America's running boom.

WAGNER COLLEGE ATHLETICS

1 Campus Road, Grymes Hill

Wagner College is the home of the 1987 NCAA Division III football national champions. The Seahawks, coached by Walt Hameline, defeated Dayton 19–3 at the Amos Alonzo Stagg Bowl in Phenix City, Alabama. The national title is part of a long and proud athletic tradition at Wagner that includes three perfect seasons in football and trips by Wagner's Division I basketball team to the NCAA Tournament (2003) and the National Invitational Tournament (1979, 2002). Rich Kotite, a Little All-American end at Wagner, went on to play as a tight end in the NFL for the New York Giants and Pittsburgh Steelers and coach the Philadelphia Eagles and the New York Jets.

SILVER LAKE GOLF COURSE

915 Victory Boulevard, Silver Lake

Silver Lake Golf Course has spawned the games of many of Staten Island's best golfers. Bill Britton, the winner of the 1989 Centel Classic on the PGA Tour and of the 2009 Senior PGA Professional Championship and the head pro at Trump National Golf Club, played at Silver Lake. Britton's brother, Bob, a six-time winner of the Staten Island Amateur, and Pete Meurer, who won thirteen Staten Island Classics and five SI Amateurs, also honed their games on Silver Lake's fairways and greens. At the eighteenth hole, a plaque commemorates the Irish immigrants who were quarantined at Tompkinsville in the 1840s and are believed, by some local historians, to be buried there.

MERRILL FIELD

Broadway and Henderson Avenue, West Brighton (Former Site)

Now home to Corporal Thompson Park, with the only public outdoor track in the borough, this site was once occupied by Merrill Field. On a dusty field with a wood-plank backstop, youngsters could play baseball all summer for ten cents—the price of a Police Athletic League (PAL) membership card. In the winter, those same youngsters played basketball in the nearby PAL Rasmussen Center.

On opening day in 1958, young Police Athletic League (PAL) ballplayers gather in front of the wooden backstop at Merrill Field in West Brighton. *Courtesy of* Staten Island Advance.

Walker Park

Bard Avenue and Delafield Place, Livingston

The Staten Island Cricket Club, the nation's oldest active cricket club, has called Walker Park home since 1886. Originally organized in 1872 by immigrants from Britain, the club featured baseball and tennis at a site in St. George. Mary Outerbridge, who introduced tennis to America in 1874, organized the first tennis tournament in America there in 1874. Walker Park also provides public facilities for tennis, softball and touch football. It is named for Randolph St. George Walker Jr., a World War I hero. Members today are primarily South Asian. The club features prominently in Joseph O'Neill's recent novel, *Netherland*.

Goodhue Center and Playground

304 Prospect Avenue, New Brighton

Goodhue Center has been a haven for children since the 1850s, when Sara Goodhue and her family opened their estate as a summer retreat for underprivileged children. In 1918, it was donated to the Children's Aid Society. Goodhue's field and playground have provided facilities for community baseball, football and basketball leagues, with volleyball and handball also available. Swimming has been an option since the Great Depression of the 1930s, when the WPA built a public pool.

Chapter 8

ENVIRONMENT

Jessica Kratz

Contributors: Chan Graham, Carrie Grassi, Eloise Hirsch and Hillel Lofaso

How pleasant were the green woods and the fields where we did stray,
Where the thorny cactus and the sunflower spread its ray;
Where we sat beneath the tree and watched the quiet blue Kill
And the haze softly settling o'er the distant Jersey hill.
—*William T. Davis, "In Memory" (1892)*

Despite the rising tide of development, Staten Island has been able to preserve and protect an amazing amount of open space. By revitalizing the waterfront, valuing the wetlands and offering multiple ways for everyone to enjoy nature, Staten Island has become "the Borough of Parks."

The nineteenth century laid the foundation for concern over development and the vision for preserving natural areas. In 1843, Thoreau visited Staten Island and wrote about its "very fine scenery." Shortly thereafter, Frederick Law Olmsted, designer of New York City's Central Park, first envisioned a greenbelt of parks while living in Eltingville. Nathaniel Lord Britton and William T. Davis founded in 1881 the SI Institute for Arts and Sciences (SIIAS, now SI Museum) to collect natural science specimens out of a concern that "the rapid growth of the community obliterated many of our most interesting natural objects." Britton and his wife, Elizabeth G. Knight Britton, were among the founders of the New York Botanical Garden in 1891.

In the twentieth century, local citizens led the charge to preserve and protect significant natural areas. If legions of concerned citizens did not work together to oppose the Willowbrook and Richmond Parkways,

Staten Island would not have the Greenbelt. The Staten Island Greenbelt Natural Areas League (SIGNAL), chaired by John Mitchell, was part of a national environmental movement, to which activists like Carlton Beil and Terence Benbow contributed. They built on efforts from the 1950s by James Whitehead and Mathilde Weingartner of SIIAS, Lynn McCracken and Richard Buegler, among others, to save what later became the Clay Pit Ponds State Park Preserve in Charleston.

Since the 1970s, Protectors of Pine Oak Woods (PPOW) has continued these protective efforts and expanded appreciation of the local environment, through monthly restoration workshops, DEC Ecology Camp scholarships and nature walks. Twenty-first-century economic decline has led to additional struggles for preservation, including the Goodhue Woods, Sharrotts Road Shorelands and Pouch Camp. Thanks to their ongoing commitments, all New Yorkers can enjoy the greenest borough of New York City.

SNUG HARBOR CHINESE SCHOLAR'S GARDEN AND BOTANICAL GARDENS

1000 Richmond Terrace, New Brighton

SEE ALSO EDUCATION AND HEALTH, THE ARTS AND ARCHITECTURE

The eighty-three-acre botanical gardens, founded in 1977, include many delights: the Chinese Scholar's Garden, the White Garden inspired by Vita Sackville-West's famous garden in Sissinghurst, England, and the Tuscan Garden modeled after Florence, Italy's Villa Gamberaia. The Connie Gretz Secret Garden, modeled after Frances Hodgson Burnett's children's classic, features a child-sized castle and a maze.

ALLISON PARK

Brentwood Avenue and Prospect Avenue, New Brighton

Allison Park was named after George W. Allison, an island resident who supervised all WPA projects on Staten Island during the Great Depression. Located in the Randall Manor section of New Brighton, its main attractions are a stone pedestrian bridge and picturesque pond, home to turtles and shorebirds. The park's flora includes American beeches, red maples, tulip trees, sensitive fern, Solomon's seal and marsh marigolds. Its pond provided drinking water for nearby Sailors' Snug Harbor until the 1939 completion of the boroughwide municipal water system.

EIBS POND PARK

Hanover Avenue and Palma Drive, Concord

Eibs Pond Park, a seventeen-acre freshwater wetland, protects New York City's largest three-acre, clay-bottomed kettle pond. It served as a water source for horses and dairy cows by the German American Eibs family in the nineteenth century and as a location to film episodes of *The Perils of Pauline* and D.W. Griffith's infamous *Birth of a Nation*. Fox Hill Golf Links included the pond as a water hazard and, when frozen, used it for curling from 1915 to 1935. An army base and Italian POW camp in the final years of World War II, the site lay vacant for nearly forty years until converted into a park.

ARTHUR VON BRIESEN PARK

SEE CIVIC AND POLITICAL LIFE

FDR BOARDWALK AND HOFFMAN AND SWINBURNE ISLANDS

Father Capodanno Boulevard, South Beach

Hoffman and Swinburne Islands, two artificial islands formed from dredged sand off South Beach, were used to quarantine infectious patients in the late 1800s. Both islands, now part of the Gateway National Recreation Area, are being turned into a refuge for birds. The islands are visible from the 2.5-mile FDR Boardwalk at South Beach. A popular resort area in the 1880s, South Beach subsequently declined in the wake of fires, water pollution and the Great Depression.

Staten Island beaches include South Beach, Midland Beach (pictured), Great Kills and Tottenville. *Courtesy of Staten Island Historical Society.*

STATEN ISLAND BLUEBELT

Throughout the Island, Especially South Shore and Mid-Island

To manage stormwater in an ecological and cost-effective manner, New York City's Department of Environmental Protection established the Staten Island Bluebelt. Upholding natural drainage corridors, such as streams, ponds and other wetland areas, the Bluebelt covers approximately one-third of Staten Island and is an aesthetic and practical alternative to the combined sewer overflows found elsewhere in the city. Starting with the Richmond Creek watershed (South Shore), these successful projects have expanded to mid-island areas and will eventually reach South Beach. Kingfisher Park in Great Kills, named for the belted kingfisher, a marine bird of prey, is part of this system.

LAST CHANCE POND PARK

Seaver and Naughton Avenues, Dongan Hills

In the mid-1960s, local residents Lou Caravone and John Mouner helped found Last Chance Pond and Wilderness Foundation to preserve these wetlands. With two saltwater marshes, a natural spring and a freshwater pond, the park is home to a diverse collection of flora and fauna. Located within a migration flyway for upstate ducks heading south, it is part of the Bluebelt, the stormwater management system.

GREAT KILLS PARK/GATEWAY NATIONAL RECREATION AREA

Hylan Boulevard, Great Kills

Great Kills (meaning "many creeks" in archaic Dutch) has always been rich in plant and animal life, with oysters especially plentiful until World War II. In 1860, John J. Crooke, a businessman and pioneering naturalist, purchased the peninsula's point. In 1929, the city bought Crooke's Point and the surrounding properties to develop into a park that took two decades to complete. In 1973, the property was transferred from city to federal jurisdiction and became part of the Gateway National Recreation Area. With a marina and barrier ocean beach, Great Kills Park's 580 acres feature thriving wildlife and recreational amenities. The recent detection of radium—stemming from the use of "sanitation controlled fill" used on the instruction of Robert Moses to save $5 million in funds in the 1930s and '40s—has led to the closure of parts of the park.

SEASIDE WILDLIFE NATURE PARK

Nelson Avenue, Tennyson Drive and Bulkhead Line, Great Kills

Once occupied by Shoals Boatyard, then a clam processing plant, this postindustrial waterfront transformed into parkland following a decade-long citizens' campaign. In 1994, Anthony and Shirlee Marraccini started Turnaround Friends, Inc., to leverage the support of private funders and elected officials. A wildflower garden, the Living Memorial Grove of Healing, native wetland species plantings and wildlife make this waterfront neighborhood park especially tranquil.

CRESCENT BEACH

Tennyson Drive, Great Kills

Frenchman Jacques Guyon settled here in 1675, and he was followed by other French and Dutch families. Oyster, clam and crab harvesting were

The workers and Swiss engineer Othmar Ammann who built the Bayonne Bridge are glorified in this 1940 WPA mural by Frederick Charles Stahr in Staten Island Borough Hall. *Courtesy of Steve White.*

Built with WPA funding as one of the first educational zoos in the United States, the Staten Island Zoo is celebrating its seventy-fifth anniversary in 2011. This photo was awarded second place in the si350 youth digital photo contest. *Courtesy of Max and Michele Saenz.*

In the 1880s, South Beach rivaled Coney Island, Brooklyn, for vaudeville shows, dancing and bathing. The Franklin D. Roosevelt Boardwalk, built with New Deal WPA funding in the 1930s and recently renovated, can still be enjoyed. *Courtesy of Elizabeth Bick.*

Staten Island's vibrant brewing and tourism industries are captured in this advertisement for Bachmann Brewing Company, with views of its Clifton factories and South Beach beer garden, circa 1890. *Courtesy of Staten Island Historical Society.*

The Staten Island Chinese School, which opened in 1969–1970, offers classes in both Mandarin and Cantonese in New Springville's I.S. 72. *Courtesy of Johnny Chin Photography.*

Along with the Tuscan Garden, the Chinese Scholar's Garden has enhanced the beauty of the historic Snug Harbor Cultural Center and Botanical Gardens. It is a must-see destination in New York City. It is utilized by the Staten Island Chinese-American Club for festivals. *Courtesy of Elizabeth Bick.*

Sri Lankan dancers and drummers, who practice at the Buddhist Vihara in Port Richmond, perform at the 2009 Samadhi festival in Princeton, New Jersey. *Courtesy of Christopher Mulé.*

Musical Chairs Chamber Ensemble, Inc., performs the world premiere of composer Andrew Sterman's (far right) "Even This Is Paradise" at the Jacques Marchais Museum of Tibetan Art. *Courtesy of Mike Shane Photography, 2010.*

Ralph Silvestro began selling Ralph's Gourmet Italian Ices in 1928 after immigrating to America from Italy. This is one of sixty thousand items in the material objects collection at the Staten Island Historical Society. *Photograph by Amessé Photography. Courtesy of Staten Island Historical Society.*

Jasper Francis Cropsey (1823–1900), a talented artist of the Hudson River School, was born on Staten Island and returned often to paint. His *Looking Oceanward from Todt Hill* (1895) is in the collection of the Staten Island Museum. *Courtesy of Staten Island Museum.*

Village of Richmond by C. Winter (1851) captures the Third County Courthouse and other homes and shops in the political center of Staten Island from 1729 to the 1898 consolidation of New York City. *Courtesy of Staten Island Museum.*

An international field of runners stream onto the Verrazano-Narrows Bridge from Fort Wadsworth, the starting point for the New York City Marathon. *Courtesy of* Staten Island Advance.

This striking image of Blue Heron Park was taken by Steven Russo of Eltingville, a Tottenville High School graduate (class of 2010) and winner in the si350 youth art contest. *Courtesy of Steven Russo.*

This circa 1910 postcard displays the Gilded Age architecture of Randall Memorial Church, the Music Hall and Neptune Fountain at Sailors' Snug Harbor. The Music Hall and the reconstructed Neptune Fountain can be visited today at Snug Harbor Culural Center and Botanical Garden. *Gift of Hugh Powell, Staten Island Museum.*

A pilgrimage site for New York City Catholics since 1936, the Our Lady of Mount Carmel Grotto continues to reflect the piety of Italian immigrants and their descendants during the annual July 16 festival and can be visited throughout the year. *Courtesy of Steve White.*

Originally called the Air Coast Defense Station, this site at New Dorp was renamed in January 1920 for Captain James E. Miller, the first American aviator killed in action for the United States in World War I. *Courtesy of Staten Island Museum.*

plentiful in the nineteenth century. Even today, the harbor provides the most bountiful clamming waters in New York state. However, these must be pasteurized commercially due to pollution, in part from its use as a landfill in the 1930s. A crescent-shaped sandbar gives the park its name.

BLUE HERON PARK

Poillon Avenue between Hylan Boulevard and Amboy Road, Annadale

Named for the four-foot-tall, grey-feathered predatory bird *Ardea herodias*, or blue heron, this park opened in 1996, after local residents had worked for three decades to preserve it. The park features Seguine Pond, one of six kettle ponds formed over fifteen thousand years ago by the retreating Wisconsin glacier, and the Friends of Blue Heron and the Urban Park Rangers provide tours of its woodlands. Remnants of a shoreline settlement known as Spanish Camp—founded in 1923 by anarchists from Spain and later home to social activist Dorothy Day, the founder of the Catholic Worker movement—can be visited. Mist nets allow for bird banding, which allows for the tracking of wild birds' migration patterns.

WOLFE'S POND PARK

Cornelia, Holten and Luten Avenues, Prince's Bay

The Wolfe's Pond Park site has been in use for over one thousand years, dating to the Native Americans. It has served as a New York City public nature preserve since 1929. Wolfe's Pond, cows, Prince's Bay, 1909. *Courtesy of Staten Island Museum.*

Over one thousand years ago, Native Americans collected shellfish at this site and on the bluffs, built longhouses, hunted turkey and cultivated corn, squash and beans. Europeans subsequently developed the oyster-harvesting industry, selling their products not only in the region but also in Europe. Farmland belonged to prominent families, such as the Johnsons, the Seguines and the Wolfes. In 1857, after the state purchased Wolfe Farm to serve as a quarantine station, local oystermen burned the facility in protest. New York City acquired the property in 1929, designated it a public nature preserve and built a dam to protect the freshwater pond.

LEMON CREEK PARK

East of Hylan Boulevard between Bayview and Richard Avenues, Prince's Bay

This 105-acre park contains a freshwater pond and one of the few purple martin bird colonies in New York City. These large swallows nest in apartment-house-style structures maintained by volunteers. The park also serves as a resting point for numerous migratory birds and, in early fall, monarch butterflies. First acquired by the NYC Parks Department in 1962, Lemon Creek Park added in 1989 the Greek Revival–style Seguine Mansion, a stately structure built in 1838 by Joseph H. Seguine, whose family made its fortune harvesting Raritan Bay oysters. A memorial plaque at the marina honors Louis Figurelli, founder of the Natural Resources Protection Association.

MOUNT LORETTO STATE UNIQUE AREA

6450 Hylan Boulevard, Pleasant Plains

SEE ALSO EDUCATION AND HEALTH, RELIGION AND SPORTS

Formed fifteen thousand years ago by a receding glacier, Mount Loretto's red cliff bluffs overlook its meadows and offer great vistas. Glossy ibis and savannah sparrows increasingly find sanctuary in its extensive grasslands. Mount Loretto also contains a substantial coastal/marine habitat filled with numerous fish and crabs. The park's tidal ponds are home to nesting egrets and wood ducks. The 194-acre park preserve was established in 1999 under the NYS Department of Environmental Conservation.

LONG POND PARK PRESERVE

Hylan Boulevard, Prince's Bay

Long Pond Preserve includes upland oak-beech woods, swamp forests, bogs and vernal ponds. This preserve is the only location in the city in which the pickerel frog (*Rana palustris*) has been observed. The park provides an important stop on the Atlantic flyway for migrating birds. Beneath the park's beech, oak and hickory trees resides an understory layer of spicebush, blueberry and many herbaceous plants. The park's bodies of water have been incorporated into the Bluebelt stormwater drainage system.

CONFERENCE HOUSE PARK

SEE CIVIC AND POLITICAL LIFE

BLOOMINGDALE PARK

Between Ramona Avenue, Bloomingdale Road and Lenevar Avenue, Rossville

With the opening of the Verrazano-Narrows Bridge in 1964, Staten Island experienced a tremendous population growth, particularly in the South Shore section. Bloomingdale Park, renovated in 2004, provided the first park ball fields south of Richmond Avenue. The NYC Parks Department also added a bocce court and soccer field, while leaving most of the 138-acre park untouched in its natural state.

CLAY PIT PONDS STATE PARK PRESERVE

83 Nielsen Avenue (Headquarters) and 2351 Veterans Road West (Interpretive Center), Charleston

If not for the efforts of local activists in the 1970s, one of the most unique habitats on Staten Island would have been lost forever. Though shaped by nearly a century of clay mining and manufacturing, Clay Pit Ponds retains the imprint of the geologic and glacial forces that formed it in the distant past. An ecosystem of ponds, marshes, clay soils and sandy hillocks supports diverse bird, amphibian, reptile and plant life. The 260-acre park is known especially for its pitch pine, Virginia pine and scrub and blackjack oak communities.

FRESHKILLS PARK

Richmond Avenue, Arthur Kill Road, the Arthur Kill River, Travis, New Springville, Arden Heights

Transforming the site of the largest landfill in the world into a productive and beautiful cultural destination offers a potent symbol of renewal and of human capacity to restore balance to the landscape. The 2,200-acre Freshkills Park will be the largest park developed in the city in over a century and rank sixth in size. In addition to more common recreational pursuits, visitors will be able to engage in mountain biking, kayaking and horseback riding in the terrain that was once a rich marsh used for harvesting salt hay and brick manufacturing. According to the parks department, "The park's design, ecological restoration and public programming will emphasize environmental sustainability and a renewed public concern for our ecological footprint."

Opened in 1947, the Fresh Kills Landfill was New York City's main sanitary landfill. It closed in 2001 and today is the focus of a landfill reclamation project to create a public park, Freshkills Park. *Courtesy of Freshkills Park.*

> ## "A National Model for Land Reuse: Freshkills Park"
>
> *Eloise Hirsch, Freshkills Park Administrator*
>
> Like the rest of New York City, Staten Island faces environmental challenges from past practices and current threats shared across the country and the world. Its unique geography—an island with wetlands and swaths of green space, forested hills and valleys—makes it the greenest of the city's boroughs. Staten Island has had to fight to retain those very assets and has been a symbol of environmental degradation as the City of New York used the salt marshes and low lands of Fresh Kills to create what became the world's largest landfill.
>
> However, Staten Island is now becoming the new face of environmental transformation, as the city turns the former landfill from liability to asset with the creation of a 2,200-acre park that will provide opportunities for research, recreation and education as it develops over the next twenty-five years. The scale of the infrastructure investments required to undergird the park is like nothing else in the country; the Fresh Kills transformation is a model being studied as cities and towns across the nation look for lessons in the reuse of lands that have been seriously compromised.
>
> Through Fresh Kills and its conversion to Freshkills Park, Staten Island has the opportunity to become a center for research and development on the full range of environmental issues cities face as they deal with sustainable land reuse. Freshkills Park will become a nationally known research station. Renewable energy, soil and water health and solutions to waste management are all issues that are integral to Fresh Kills' past and Freshkills Park's future. With the addition of Freshkills Park's acreage to the Staten Island Greenbelt, Staten Island will build on its green strengths as it becomes an icon for sustainable solutions to urban environmental problems.

Visy Paper Recycling

4435 Victory Boulevard, Travis

In 1997, Pratt Industries' Visy Paper subsidiary opened this $200 million paper mill, using a significant portion of New York City's waste paper as its raw material. It was the first major manufacturing facility built in the city since World War II and the first to use the state's "brownfields" program for the redevelopment of old industrial property. Pratt Industries (USA) added a new materials recovery facility and box-making plant in 2008, an important component of the city's recycling program.

WILLIAM T. DAVIS WILDLIFE REFUGE

Trail Access near Travis and Mulberry Avenues, Travis

In the 1920s, William T. Davis, one of Staten Island's preeminent naturalists and founder of the Staten Island Institute of Arts and Sciences (SIIAS), contacted the Audubon Society to solicit support for procuring and operating a bird sanctuary on Staten Island. With land obtained from the former Staten Island Water Supply Company and Crystal Water Company, the sanctuary opened in 1933. In the 1950s, SIIAS revitalized, expanded and named the sanctuary. Its well-marked trail, with observation platforms, offers views of the outlying marshes and a glimpse into the future Freshkills Park.

LATOURETTE PARK AND GOLF COURSE

Naturalist and historian William T. Davis, cofounder of the Staten Island Institute of Arts and Sciences (now the Staten Island Museum), was an early advocate of preserving the island's green spaces. *Courtesy of Staten Island Museum.*

1001 Richmond Hill Road, New Springville
Greenbelt Nature Center, 700 Rockland Avenue, Egbertville

Comprised of Buck's Hollow, Heyerdahl Hill and its golf course, the 511-acre LaTourette Park is part of the 2,800-acre Greenbelt. Threatened by Robert Moses's plans for Richmond and Willowbrook Parkways, the park remained intact and is now home to the Greenbelt Nature Center, which welcomes twenty thousand visitors annually. The nature center offers a variety of programs and exhibits, as well as access to the hiking trails of the Greenbelt. The park's size affords a diversity of forest habitats and supports considerable biodiversity.

WILLOWBROOK PARK

Victory Boulevard at Morani Street, Willowbrook

This popular park has natural wilderness alongside ball fields, hiking trails, an archery range, a five-acre lake and the Carousel for All Children. For centuries, the area flowed with streams and waterways, later utilized to power a sawmill. The Staten Island Water Company sold the city the initial parkland in 1909, and the park itself opened in 1929 and subsequently took on additional acreage intended for the unconstructed Willowbrook Parkway.

JOSEPH MANNA PARK

Forest Avenue and Goethals Road North, Old Place

Acquired by the parks department in 1991, this site was named for Seaman First Class Radioman Joseph Manna (1924–1942), who served and died on the U.S. Navy destroyer USS *Duncan* during World War II. An immigrant from Licignano, Italy, and a graduate of Port Richmond High School, Manna fell during the infamous Battle of Guadalcanal. Created through the initiative of the Mariners Harbor Civic Association, this small triangle-shaped park also honors a number of other fallen veterans of World Wars I and II (Edward A. Bloom, Harry A. Gill, Constantine Busso and Frank Busso). An additional plaque commemorates the workers for the Port Authority of New York and New Jersey who fell in World War II.

GRANITEVILLE SWAMP PARK/ OLD PLACE CREEK WETLANDS

Goethals Road North, Meeker Avenue, Morrow Street, Graniteville

From 1841 to 1896, a quarry at this site yielded stone thought to be granite, but it was recently identified as a crystallized stone called trap rock. The park area has a unique geological formation containing rare igneous rocks, such as xenolith and trondhjemite, and an unusually varied ecology of swamp, upland forest, marshes and creeks. An important site for wading birds, Graniteville Swamp has been designated an area of protection by the Harbor Herons Wildlife Refuge. The headwaters for the seventy-acre Old Place Creek wetlands begin here and meander toward the Goethals Bridge, providing a wonderful stretch of tidal salt marsh, a rich and biologically diverse ecosystem.

SAW MILL CREEK MARSH

Chelsea Road between Gulf Avenue and River Road, Chelsea

This site surrounds a briny creek that empties into the Arthur Kill behind Prall's Island. In its salt marshes, the Lenape grew corn, squash and beans and harvested oysters from the creek. In the 1700s, Richard Merrill built a gristmill to make flour from grain grown on local farms and a sawmill to make lumber. By the 1850s, oysters were freshened in the creek mud flats. Since the city made the marsh a park in 1994, egrets, herons, falcons and eastern cottontail rabbits have made it their home.

HIGH ROCK PARK

200 Nevada Avenue, Egbertville

The vast natural area later designated as the Greenbelt was born at High Rock Park. Six years before the first Earth Day in 1970, the threatened destruction of High Rock triggered Staten Island's environmental movement. Following the 1964 completion of the Staten Island Expressway, a developer announced plans to build apartments on the grounds of the

Site of the High Rock Girl Scout Camp from 1951 to 1964, High Rock Park is now a part of the Greenbelt. Here are some Girl Scouts at High Rock Park. *Courtesy of Staten Island Historical Society.*

former High Rock Girl Scout Camp. A committed group of citizens, led by Gretta Moulton, campaigned to purchase High Rock. Today, a gate erected in 1995 commemorates her accomplishment, and a rustic stone house holds the Greenbelt Conservancy headquarters.

PROTECTORS OF PINE OAK WOODS

SEE CIVIC AND POLITICAL LIFE

OHRBACH LAKE

1465 Manor Road, Manor Heights

Surrounded entirely by the Greenbelt, Ohrbach Lake covers approximately 17 acres of the 143-acre Pouch Camp, the property of the Boy Scouts of America. In the 1940s, the now-defunct Ohrbach's department store funded a dam that allowed flow from adjacent ponds to expand the lake. Forty thousand visitors swim, canoe and kayak here annually, notably Scouts and YMCA campers. Composer Irving Berlin, who donated the proceeds of "God Bless America" to the New York Scouts, has a lodge named after him that overlooks the lake.

REED'S BASKET WILLOW SWAMP

Ocean Terrace and Merrick Avenue, Dongan Hills/Todt Hill

In the early 1800s, John Reed planted purple willow trees for use in weaving baskets. This highly specialized occupation, common among Staten Islanders, involved harvesting tree bark, peeling and soaking it in water before weaving. The 47.8-acre area, accessed by the Greenbelt's Yellow Trail, includes three ponds, a swamp and a forest with varied species of trees, though mostly young oak.

CLOVE LAKES PARK

1150 Clove Road, West New Brighton

SEE ALSO MILITARY HISTORY AND SPORTS

Ice skating at Cleve Lakes Park, as at other local ponds, was a favorite winter pastime. Pictured here are skaters at Historic Richmond Town. *Courtesy of Staten Island Historical Society.*

The two-hundred-acre Clove Lakes Park features three bodies of water—Clove Lake, Martlings Pond (now Richmond Pond) and Brooks Pond—and a giant 146-foot-tall, three-hundred-year-old tulip tree. Clove Lake derives its name from the Dutch *kloven* (meaning "cleft"), the valley between the steep slopes of Emerson and Grymes Hills. The lakes formed from dams placed on the creek that once held a gristmill and served as a local water source. The parks department borough headquarters are here, and it serves as a major destination for outdoors fishing, hiking, birding, skating, 5K races and other sports.

Silver Lake Park and Golf Course

Victory Boulevard, Tompkinsville

This 1896 image captures Silver Lake before it was drained and converted into a reservoir, used from 1913 to 1971. *Courtesy of Staten Island Historical Society.*

Intending to create a local version of Central Park and Prospect Park, Staten Island writer John De Morgan appealed in 1900 to the state assembly to acquire land around the lake. Long used for boating, casinos and ice harvesting, in 1897, the park hosted the National Skating Amateur Championship races. Silver Lake was drained in 1913 and converted to a reservoir, the endpoint of the Catskill water supply system for New York City. An underground storage facility replaced the reservoir in 1971.

Chapter 9

CIVIC AND POLITICAL LIFE

James Kaser

*Contributors: Jeffrey Coogan, Rachel Jirka,
Barnett Shepherd and Amy Stempler*

On Staten Island, politics and civic life have often focused on issues of identity and rights. During the colonial period, islanders sought military protection and struggled to get funds for basic internal improvements, namely a county seat and roads. By the mid-nineteenth century, civil and political activism by islanders attracted national attention, as in the 1856 running of the first Republican Party presidential campaign or the 1858 burning of the quarantine station. A vocal and visible minority supported the expansion of rights through the abolition of slavery and women's suffrage, drawing Susan B. Anthony to the island's shores. Despite this, Staten Islanders joined others throughout New York City in opposing Abraham Lincoln's election. By the 1890s, National Prohibition Park (now Westerleigh Park) drew future president Theodore Roosevelt and the outspoken populist William Jennings Bryan to support temperance as moral reform.

Two important statewide changes that affected politics were the 1827 abolition of slavery and the 1846 constitution that gave all male citizens over age twenty-one the vote and a greater voice. But, arguably, the most significant shift came in 1894, when Staten Island residents voted nearly four to one in favor of consolidation with the city. When it took effect in 1898, the construction of a new Borough Hall, courthouse and civic center confirmed a shift in the center of gravity from Richmond to the North Shore.

In the twentieth century, grass-roots organizations engaged in campaigns to save historical sites and natural resources. Robert Moses's Willowbrook Parkway plan was thwarted by citizen activists who saved a parcel of woodland, leading to the creation of the 2,800-acre Greenbelt. Committed volunteers prevented the leveling of architecturally significant buildings at Snug Harbor and established a cultural center and botanical gardens. Citizen protests and a parent-sponsored lawsuit closed down the Willowbrook State School, a facility for the developmentally disabled. After decades of agitation, local politicians forced the closure of Fresh Kills Landfill in 2001, a waste-treatment facility created in 1948 that became the largest in the world.

Despite these victories, the island lost considerable political power under a new city charter, leading to an overwhelming vote for secession in 1993 that was thwarted by city and state representatives. These twentieth-century efforts to maintain Staten Island's traditional character and claim the financial resources to which the borough is entitled have created a distinctive identity for the island.

Former vice presidents Daniel Tompkins and Aaron Burr lived here, but the island has often been visited by national political leaders, including Presidents John Adams, Thomas Jefferson, Andrew Jackson, Ulysses S. Grant, Franklin D. Roosevelt, Theodore Roosevelt, John F. Kennedy, Richard Nixon, George H.W. Bush and William J. Clinton. The island has also nurtured other nationally significant figures, including Arthur Von Briesen, first president of the Legal Aid Society; Anning S. Prall, chairman of the Federal Communications Commission (FCC); Edward R. Stettinius, secretary of state under President Franklin Roosevelt; and Jeb McGruder, top aide to President Nixon. Of more significance to the daily life of island residents are the political meetings, the activities of civic organizations, military and ethnic parades, picnics and cultural celebrations. These forms of participatory democracy involve the island's growing population in civic life throughout the borough and well beyond it.

Borough Hall

10 Richmond Terrace, St. George

Completed in 1906, Staten Island Borough Hall's sophisticated design and location at the closest point to Manhattan celebrate the island's 1898 consolidation with New York City and signify the ascendency of St. George

A 1910 postcard depicts Staten Island's Borough Hall a decade after the political center of Staten Island was moved from Richmond to St. George. *Courtesy of the Norman L. Jeffers Historical Postcard Collection, Archives & Special Collections, Department of the Library, College of Staten Island, CUNY.*

as the island's civic center. Architect John M. Carrère, a resident of St. George and partner in the Manhattan firm Carrère and Hastings, worked closely with borough president George Cromwell to select the site. By far the largest structure on Staten Island in 1906, the building has two fronts. The island side juts forward from the wings and offers a massive base for the clock tower. The style, a tall mansard roof with dormers and classical details, red brick and limestone, relates to seventeenth-century French architecture. In the lobby, Frederick Charles Stahr painted a series of WPA murals, depicting turning points in local history. Landmarked in 1982, the building has thus far housed the administrations of fourteen borough presidents.

120TH POLICE PRECINCT STATION HOUSE

78 Richmond Terrace, St. George

Constructed as the 66th Precinct Station House, this neo-Renaissance building was designed by James Whitford Sr. (1871–1947), "the dean of Staten Island architects," in 1920. Its 1923 opening was marked by a parade

Mounted police in New Dorp's 80th Precinct in 1890, thirty-three years after the Metropolitan Police Department was founded. *Courtesy of Staten Island Museum.*

and speeches by borough president John A. Lynch and police commissioner Richard Enright. The building became the 120th Precinct when all the police precincts in the city were renumbered in 1929 and was designated a landmark in 1982.

SEAMEN'S SOCIETY FOR CHILDREN AND FAMILIES

50 Bay Street, St. George

The Seamen's Society for Children and Families is one of the oldest charities on Staten Island. The agency was founded in 1846 to provide healthcare and education assistance to the impoverished children of seamen. Over time, the society grew to include foster care and boarding homes for nearly five hundred children, as well as offering child abuse and domestic violence prevention programs. The society is now headquartered in a five-story building in St. George, where it continues its mission as the largest child welfare service provider based on the island.

ST. GEORGE POST OFFICE

45 Bay Street, St. George

Built in 1932, the St. George Post Office remains an important facility for postal service on Staten Island. That service was consolidated as the Staten Island General Post Office in 1917. This building included offices for the United States Civil Service, the FBI and the United States Customs Bureau. About 125,000 letters are mailed on Staten Island daily, with the branch at 550 Manor Road now serving as the main post office.

THE STATEN ISLAND LGBT CENTER

25 Victory Boulevard, Tompkinsville

Since the early 1970s, Staten Islanders have been involved in the national LGBT movement, including through the Gay Activists Alliance. Their efforts were continued in the 1980s by Lambda Associates of Staten Island, the Staten Island Lesbian Kinship (SILK) and the Staten Island AIDS Task Force, renamed Community Health Action of Staten Island (CHASI) in 2004. The 1990s brought even greater advocacy and demonstrations, as in the 1992 debate on NYC's Children of the Rainbow curriculum. In 2005, the first Gay Pride Parade kicked off on Staten Island, and the LGBT Center was organized by CHASI. In 2007, Matthew Titone became the first openly gay elected official on Staten Island (Sixty-first District).

DANIEL D. TOMPKINS/TOMPKINSVILLE

Victory Boulevard at Bay Street, Tompkinsville

Daniel D. Tompkins (1774-1825) served as governor of New York from 1807 to 1817 and as vice president of the United States under President James Monroe. During the War of 1812, Tompkins was appointed commander of the Third District Militia, which covered southern New York and parts of New England. He was committed to the war, using personal funds for troops and equipment when support from the state assembly waned. As governor, Tompkins was reelected three times, allowing him to accomplish a number of liberal reforms, including the gradual emancipation of enslaved Africans in New York state. Tompkins settled in Staten Island in 1812, where he founded the village of Tompkinsville and established a steam ferry business between Staten Island and Manhattan.

EDGEWATER VILLAGE HALL

111 Canal Street, Stapleton

A New York City landmark, the Edgewater Village Hall was built in the Romanesque Revival style in 1889 by Paul Kuhne, a Stapleton architect of German birth. It served as the courthouse and civic center for Edgewater Village, which included Tompkinsville, Stapleton and Clifton. At that time and until 1898, five townships—Northfield, Southfield, Westfield, Castleton and Middletown—and four incorporated villages—Edgewater, New Brighton, Port Richmond and Tottenville—each had their own government. In the twentieth century, Edgewater Village Hall housed a police court, a bank and the Board of Health. Originally part of the farm where Cornelius Vanderbilt grew up,

"THE NAACP: FAMILY TIES AND CIVIC LEADERSHIP"

Dolores N. Morris, Five-Time Emmy Award–Winning TV Producer/Writer

Dear Staten Island,

Congratulations!

My family has been here for five generations. I am descended from oyster fishermen, teachers, artists, sheriffs, entrepreneurs and community activists.

I am related to the last slave sold on Staten Island and the most successful African American businessman on the eastern seaboard.

My grandfather, William A. Morris, built a flourishing moving business from a horse and wagon to moving vans and warehouses. I.S. 61 is named for him, and it celebrates not only his business success but his lifelong community service. He founded the Staten Island branch of the NAACP, pioneering the cause of equality for all of us.

My aunt, Evelyn King, was an innovative educator and island historian. I am surrounded by relatives who, like myself, came through your public schools and went on to higher education and service to the community.

I have taken your ferries a thousand times, played in your parks and beaches, spent endless childhood hours at your zoo and ridden your horses though the tree-lined trails of Clove Lakes Park.

Thank you, Staten Island, for being the different borough. Thank you for your diverse population, your mixture of languages, cultures, religions and political beliefs. We are all different, and yet we are one, in Staten Island. Here's to the next 350 years as we celebrate our glorious differences together.

the land surrounding the Village Hall was formerly called Washington Park but renamed in 1934 to honor James J. Tappen, a Stapleton resident killed during World War I.

STATEN ISLAND NAACP/NY URBAN LEAGUE

69 Wright Street, Stapleton; 6 Van Duzer Street, Tompkinsville

William Morris founded the Staten Island chapter of the NAACP in 1925 in response to attacks on the home of an African American resident. Morris, a third-generation Staten Islander and owner of his own moving company, is the namesake of I.S. 61 in Castleton and an annual civic award given out by the Staten Island NAACP. The chapter, presided by Edward Josey, has worked long and tirelessly to fulfill the organization's mission of equality for and tolerance of all citizens. Staten Island's chapter of the New York Urban League was launched in 1964 to tackle a wide range of health, housing, economic and educational issues.

COMMUNITY BOARDS

CB1: 1 Edgewater Plaza, Clifton
CB2: 460 Brielle Avenue, Manor Heights
CB3: 655–218 Rossville Avenue, Woodrow

Staten Island's three community boards (1, 2 and 3) serve as representatives and advocates for the residents of their respective districts. Community boards have an important advisory role in land use, zoning laws and any other issue that affects the welfare and quality of life of a community. The boards are made up of civic-minded residents, half of whom are appointed by the borough president and half appointed by the district's city council member. The three districts roughly encompass the northern (1), central (2) and southern (3) sections of the island.

REPUBLICAN PARTY NATIONAL HEADQUARTERS

Bay Street and Simonson (now Greenfield) Avenue, Clifton (Former Site)

In the mid-1850s, the Republican Party arose in the wake of the imploding Whig Party and in clear opposition to the expansion of slavery. John C. Fremont (1813–1890), the "Pathfinder" and periodic Staten Island resident, ran as its first presidential candidate in 1856. The party's rented office space in Clifton became the unofficial national headquarters, where reportedly thousands of federal office seekers came, where Fremont possibly lived during the campaign and where he learned of his loss to James Buchanan. On Staten Island, Fremont polled third, behind both Buchanan and Know-Nothing anti-Catholic candidate and ex-president Millard Fillmore. Fremont returned to Staten Island in retirement, where he lived until his death in 1890.

Arthur Von Briesen Park

Bay Street, Shore Acres

This landscaped waterfront park, with stately oak, horse chestnut and tulip trees, sits on the former farming estate of Arthur Von Briesen (1843–1920), cofounder and first president from 1890 to 1916 of the Legal Aid Society. He expanded the limited mission of the German Legal Aid Society to form a model institution that was duplicated across the nation, protecting all immigrants regardless of birth or nationality. Von Briesen named the property overlooking the Narrows *Gernda*, German for "wishing to be there." His friend and fellow Republican President Theodore Roosevelt addressed letters to him at "First House on the Left, America." In 1945, his heirs donated the land to the parks department.

Oude Dorp

See Ethnicity and Immigration

Thomas Dongan/Cassiltowne

Dongan Avenue, Castleton Corners

As governor of New York from 1682 until 1688, Thomas Dongan (1634–1715) presided over the colonial assembly responsible for the "Charter of Liberties," the document defining political and religious rights of the provincial government in New York. In 1687, Dongan acquired 5,100 acres on Staten Island. Adjacent to Port Richmond, he built a manor home called the "Lordshippe or Manner of Cassiltowne," from whence the name Castleton Corners was derived. Dongan Avenue and Dongan Hills both commemorate this historic figure.

Protectors of Pine Oak Woods

Greenbelt, Egbertville

Since the early 1970s, Protectors of Pine Oak Woods has been Staten Island's largest environmental conservation advocacy group. Along with Waterfront Watch and the Staten Island Citizens Planning Committee, these organizations

Assemblywoman
Elizabeth Connelly
and Assemblyman Eric
Vitaliano met with
wetlands preservation
activists in 1987. *Courtesy of
Archives & Special Collections,
Department of the Library,
College of Staten Island,
CUNY.*

reflect the environmental activism characteristic of the local political culture since the early 1900s. These groups have achieved major successes, including the addition of thousands of acres to Staten Island's park system and the prevention of a proposal to extend Richmond Parkway through the Greenbelt.

HISTORIC RICHMOND TOWN'S THIRD COUNTY COURTHOUSE

302 Center Street, Richmond

The Third County Courthouse, built in 1837 in the Greek Revival style, was Staten Island's first significant county building. Richmond became the county seat in 1729 with the opening of its initial courthouse, which was subsequently destroyed by the British during the Revolutionary War. Replacing a second structure that was in use for less than fifty years, the Third County Courthouse remained in service until 1919, when the court moved to the new county seat, St. George. The courthouse is currently used as the Visitor Center at Historic Richmond Town. In St. George, construction began in 2008 on a new state Supreme Court building.

HISTORIC RICHMOND TOWN'S CHRISTOPHER HOUSE

Off Arthur Kill Road, Richmond

Named for Joseph Christopher, its owner during the Revolutionary War, this fieldstone house was likely used as a meeting place for the island's

Committee of Public Safety. The circa 1720 house was originally located on the Cassiltowne estate of colonial governor Thomas Dongan and was relocated from 819 Willowbrook Road to the Historic Richmond Town in the 1970s.

THE CONFERENCE HOUSE

298 Saterlee Street, Tottenville

Overlooking the Arthur Kill and Perth Amboy, New Jersey, and home to the Billopp family for four generations, this was the largest house on Staten Island when British naval officer Christopher Billopp (died 1724) built it circa 1680. The house's walls were assembled from stones gathered on the beach. The symmetrical façade and central hall plan are British, while the parapet end walls are Dutch. Later, Christopher Billopp (1737–1827) became Staten Island's leading Loyalist who commanded the local militia called Billopp's Brigade during the American Revolution. On September 11, 1776, Billopp hosted an unsuccessful peace conference between American Patriots John Adams, Benjamin Franklin and Edward Rutledge and British admiral Richard Lord Howe. The failure of the talks led to the continuation of the American Revolution for seven years, after which Colonel Billopp and his family migrated to Nova Scotia, Canada. There, he became a political leader in the newly incorporated city of St. John, New Brunswick, Canada. Today, the house is the centerpiece of Conference House Park, which also celebrates the 3.3-acre site's equally rich Lenape history.

The Conference House, also known as the Billopp House, was the site where Benjamin Franklin, John Adams and Edward Rutledge affirmed America's desire for freedom and independence at the start of the American Revolution. *Courtesy of Staten Island Museum.*

ARTHUR KILL CORRECTIONAL FACILITY

2911 Arthur Kill Road, Charleston

Originally housing a drug rehabilitation center, the Arthur Kill Correctional Facility opened as a medium-security prison in 1976. Operated by the New York State Department of Correctional Services, the all-male prison is the only correctional facility on Staten Island. The Old Red Jail in Coccles Town (now Historic Richmond Town), one of the earliest prisons on Staten Island, was built in 1710 and included a whipping post.

JOHN J. MARCHI PAPERS

2800 Victory Boulevard, CSI Archives, Willowbrook

Senator Marchi with group protesting the wetland condemnation of land on February 10, 1987. *Courtesy of Archives & Special Collections, Department of the Library, College of Staten Island, CUNY.*

Elected in 1956, Republican John J. Marchi (1921–2009) served in the New York Senate until 2006, the longest-tenured legislator in any level of government in the country. Marchi chaired the Finance Committee during the city's fiscal crisis in the 1970s, introduced successful legislation requiring the closure of the Fresh Kills Landfill and led Staten Island's secession movement in the early 1990s, for which he was probably best known. Marchi was committed to preserving local cultural institutions and helped establish the College of Staten Island, CUNY. The donation of his papers, which mirror every issue important to the borough's residents, laid the foundation for the college's archives.

Elizabeth A. Connelly Center

930 Willowbrook Road, Willowbrook

Assemblywoman Elizabeth A. Connelly (1928–2006), elected in 1973, was the first woman from Staten Island elected to public office. Connelly also became the first female Democrat to chair a standing New York Assembly committee, and in 1995, she served as speaker *pro tempore*, the highest leadership position ever held by a woman in the assembly. Connelly was committed to addressing mental health, developmental disabilities and substance abuse issues, as well as environmental affairs. Connelly retired in 2000 as the longest-serving woman in the history of the New York legislature. Her legacy continues with the Elizabeth A. Connelly Center, dedicated to serving those with developmental disabilities.

Project Hospitality

100 Park Avenue, Port Richmond

Founded in 1982, Project Hospitality is a community-based, not-for-profit volunteer agency dedicated to serving Staten Island's homeless population. The group initially opened the borough's first emergency homeless shelter and subsequently established a trailer that provided emergency and referral services at the Staten Island Ferry terminal, the only heated public space on the island. Soon the organization grew to offer services for the poor, hungry and those living with multiple diagnoses, such as HIV, substance abuse and mental illness. Project Hospitality serves more than five thousand residents each year and remains the only comprehensive homeless service provider on Staten Island.

Lenape Treaty Site

Bay Street and Victory Boulevard, Tompkinsville

On April 13, 1670, representatives of the Lenape tribe and Francis Lovelace, governor general of the New York colony, met and signed a treaty at the Watering Place, Tompkinsville. By the terms of the agreement, the Lenape surrendered ownership of Staten Island to the English in exchange for four hundred fathoms of wampum (trade beads), thirty boots, thirty shirts, twenty kettles, twenty hoes, sixty barrels of shot and a keg of powder, among other items. Staten Island had been "sold" by the Lenape several times before, but the 1670 treaty is considered the final and authoritative renunciation of ownership by the native peoples.

1ˢᵗ FDNY STATEN ISLAND FIREHOUSE

1189 Castleton Avenue, Port Richmond

Thirty-five volunteer fire companies protected Staten Island in 1896 and embodied the vibrancy of civic life in the late nineteenth century. One of these, the Medora Hook and Ladder Company No. 3, erected its West Brighton firehouse around 1885. Following the 1898 consolidation with New York City, the FDNY began to provide financial support for the volunteer companies until they could be replaced with paid, professional units. In 1905, the city purchased the Medora building, which became the FDNY's first firehouse on Staten Island, and it continues its service today as home of Ladder 79 and Battalion 22.

SWAN HOTEL, RICHMOND TERRACE

Richmond Terrace, New Brighton (Former Site)

The Swan Hotel in New Brighton was the scene of a massive celebration in 1827 to observe the end of slavery in New York state. Fireworks, picnics and speeches over two days marked the end of a long legislative process in the state, beginning after the American Revolution. Although this earlier legislation emancipated African Americans, young people born between 1799 and 1827 were still required to serve long periods of indenture. The final removal of slavery occurred in 1841, when the state legislature abolished a provision enabling nonresidents to own slaves for up to nine months. The Swan Hotel was built circa 1792 and survived into the twentieth century.

PEACE ACTION AT THE UNITARIAN CHURCH

312 Fillmore Street, New Brighton

In the early 1940s, the Staten Island Youth Council organized the first stirrings of antiwar activism. During the Vietnam War, the Reverend George McClain led the Staten Island Peace Coalition. Violence in Central

America in the 1980s brought renewed activism, while two chapters of the National Committee for a Sane Nuclear Policy (SANE) protested nuclear buildups. In 1983, Pete Seeger and Tom Chapin performed at the future site of the Stapleton home port in a concert organized by the Committee for a Nuclear-Free Island. In 2002, with the invasion of Iraq months away, over forty residents met at the Unitarian Church to form a chapter of Peace Action of Staten Island (PASI), in collaboration with the Unitarian Social Concerns Committee, Pax Christi, People Against Oppression and War and the Staten Island Greens. PASI organizes voter and letter-writing campaigns as well as forums, vigils and the annual Peace and Freedom Festivals in Tappen Park, Stapleton.

GEORGE CURTIS HOME

Davis and Henderson Avenues, West Brighton

A well-known author, journalist and reformer, George Curtis (1824–1892) wrote for and later became editor of the influential *Harper's Weekly*. A prominent orator on behalf of the abolitionist cause, he also worked for the advancement of women's suffrage, Native American rights, public education and civil service reform, serving as president of the National Civil Service Reform League. He participated in the founding of the Republican Party in 1856 and stumped for its first presidential candidate, John C. Fremont. Curtis married Anna Shaw, sister of Colonel Robert Gould Shaw, commander of the Fifty-fourth Massachusetts Infantry Regiment, portrayed in the 1989 film *Glory*. His daughter, Elizabeth, led the Women's Political Equality Club of Staten Island.

George William Curtis, circa 1860, and his daughter, Elizabeth Curtis, promoted women's rights throughout New York state. *Courtesy of Brady-Handy Collection, Library of Congress Prints and Photographs Division. Washington, D.C., and Staten Island Museum.*

Parade Route

Forest Avenue, Castleton

Forest Avenue, Port Richmond Avenue and Hylan Boulevard all were common routes for parades, led initially by volunteer fire companies and veterans groups celebrating civic, patriotic and ethnic pride. Flag Day parades were particularly popular. Since 1909, Staten Islanders have recognized their Italian heritage with the Columbus Day Parade. More recently, since 2005 and 2007, respectively, the Gay Pride Parade and the Black Heritage Parade have been initiated. The year 2010 marked the 46th annual St. Patrick's Day Parade, the 91st annual Memorial Day Parade, both on Forest Avenue, and the 100th anniversary of Independence Day Parade in Travis.

Rotary Club of Staten Island

LiGreci's Staaten, 697 Forest Avenue, West Brighton

The Rotary Club of Staten Island was founded in 1921 and has maintained its own charitable foundation since 1962. Committed to the mission set forth by Rotary International, the Rotary Club of Staten Island has a long tradition of community service, both at home and abroad. Staten Islanders subsequently chartered four additional local Rotary Clubs: South Shore (1955), North Shore (1957), Mid-Island (1990) and Gateway (1991).

Prohibition Park

Clinton Fiske Avenue at the Boulevard (University Temple), Westerleigh

In 1887, the National Prohibition Campground Association purchased twenty-five acres in the neighborhood of Westerleigh and established a facility replete with fields for tents, sports and speeches. Known as Prohibition Park, the site became a summer destination for followers of the temperance movement and the Prohibition Party. There they engaged in recreational activities, attended religious services, listened to lectures about the evils of alcohol and strategized for political campaigns to impose a legal ban. Most of the streets in the community were named after prominent Prohibition

Prohibition Park Auditorium, a four-thousand-seat theater within the summer retreat, hosted speakers promoting the temperance movement as well as an important rally in 1894 for the consolidation of New York City. *Courtesy of Staten Island Historical Society.*

leaders or for states where support for the Prohibition Party was strongest. The prohibitionists subsequently erected University Temple, a four-thousand-seat auditorium that, in 1894, held a huge rally for proponents of consolidation with New York City.

STATEN ISLAND FIREFIGHTERS MEMORIAL

Clove Road and Targee Street, Concord

Community advocacy and leadership produced this affecting monument to fallen firefighters. Claiming one of the largest retired firefighters organizations in the country, Staten Island did not have its own firefighters' memorial before 1993. With strong financial support from the community, a committee of retired and active firefighters found a way to honor the 114 firefighters from the borough who have fallen in the line of duty since 1865.

Chapter 10

ARCHITECTURE

Barnett Shepherd

Small stone farmhouses from the seventeenth and eighteenth centuries, nineteenth-century hilltop mansions and twentieth-century housing developments exhibit the great variety of American architectural forms found on Staten Island. The features and beauty of Staten Island's churches, institutions and civic buildings reflect its citizens' knowledge of the larger world and pride in their communities.

Staten Island's buildings illustrate strong ties to the surrounding region and nation. Farmhouses built by early Huguenot, Dutch and English settlers bear similarities to buildings of other Lower Hudson River Valley communities, and these earliest structures reflect the techniques of their builders' native European cultures. Beginning in the early nineteenth century, Staten Island's architecture illustrates the story of American suburban development. The prosperous businessmen who developed New Brighton and Clifton on the North Shore called upon leading architects of the New York City area to design their residences. Local builders utilized nationally published plan books throughout the nineteenth century, and architects Otto Loeffler in Stapleton and Edward Alfred Sargent in Clifton designed many fine buildings.

After Staten Island became a borough in 1898, New York City chose leading architects to design Borough Hall, courthouses and libraries. Several architects of national prominence lived on Staten Island, including John Merven Carrère of Carrère & Hastings and Ernest Flagg, who had a weekend residence here. In Arrochar, H.H. Richardson built the first residence he lived in as a married man. William H. Mersereau of Oakwood designed Manhattan's reconstructed Fraunces Tavern and other restorations in Delaware and Virginia.

Several unique characteristics of Staten Island's historic architecture set it apart from the region and nation. In the nineteenth century, the early and frequent deployment of porches and towers responds to the picturesque qualities of its hillside and waterfront terrain. The use of local stone and granite distinguishes many Staten Island buildings. Into the twentieth century, the preference for narrow three-bay houses on subdivided property resulted from the high value of land and the need to achieve a maximum return.

The Staten Island 9/11 *Postcards* Memorial was designed by Japanese American Masayuki Sono. It was dedicated on September 11, 2004, before an audience of three thousand people. *Courtesy of Elizabeth Bick.*

STATEN ISLAND 9/11 MEMORIAL

North Shore Waterfront Esplanade, St. George

This striking waterfront memorial to the victims of the September 11, 2001 terrorist attack that destroyed the World Trade Center was designed by New York City architect Masayuki Sono (born 1971). Named *Postcards*, the design was selected in 2003 from 179 submissions in a worldwide competition. A native of Kobe, Japan, and survivor of the 1995 earthquake there, Sono was a resident of New York City when the attack occurred. For his design, Sono multiplied the dimensions of a postcard by 267 to convey the scale of the loss, as 267 of the 9/11 victims were from Staten Island. He remarked, "The concept for this memorial came from a desire to create something that would connect us all to the victims of this tragedy. I chose the symbol of the postcard because we all write to people we remember and miss." Three thousand people attended the September 11, 2004 dedication ceremony.

STATEN ISLAND BOROUGH HALL
SEE CIVIC AND POLITICAL LIFE

U.S. LIGHTHOUSE SERVICE DEPOT

1 Lighthouse Plaza, St. George

The Lighthouse Service depot complex was established for the storage of materials destined for East Coast lighthouses and as an experimental station for the testing of new materials and methods of lighthouse operation. The most prominent building on the waterfront site was constructed around 1868. A boldly detailed granite and red brick office building, it was designed in the Second Empire style by A.B. Mullett, supervising architect of the U.S. Treasury. This "fireproof" structure held the depot's records. Wings were added in 1901, and it later became the U.S. Coast Guard Station Administration Building.

ST. GEORGE HISTORIC DISTRICT

St. George

The St. George Historic District includes portions of St. Mark's Place, Carroll Place, Westervelt Avenue, Hamilton Avenue, the Phelps Place cul-de-sac and short stretches of Richmond Terrace. Part of a larger suburban development, it contains some seventy-eight buildings mostly constructed in the late nineteenth century. The oldest structure is the house at 404 Richmond Terrace, now called the Pavilion on the Terrace. The district has its roots in New Brighton, one of the metropolitan area's earliest planned suburban communities, and is notable for the large number of residences designed by Staten Island architect Edward Alfred Sargent (1842–1914).

ST. PAUL'S AVENUE/STAPLETON HEIGHTS HISTORIC DISTRICT

Stapleton

St. Paul's Avenue curves midway around the sides of Ward Hill and Grymes Hill, linking the villages of Tompkinsville and Stapleton. The historic district is a neighborhood of single-family homes, some dating to the early nineteenth century. Many were designed by Otto Loeffler (1862–1930) and other Stapleton builders. The avenue is named for St. Paul's Memorial Church (Episcopal), which was established by the Caleb T. Ward family, the large landowner of the area. Beginning in the 1880s, the success of Stapleton's lager breweries attracted families of German background. Brewer George Bechtel built the large Queen Anne–style house at 387 St. Paul's Avenue for his daughter.

EDGEWATER VILLAGE HALL

SEE CIVIC AND POLITICAL LIFE

ALICE AUSTEN HOUSE

SEE THE ARTS

ST. JOHN'S CHURCH

1331 Bay Street, Clifton

The tower and steeple of this imposing light-brown granite church are visible from the Narrows. Modeled after "Shakespeare's church," Holy Trinity Church in Stratford-upon-Avon, England, St. John's was designed for an Episcopal congregation by Arthur D. Gilman (1821–1882) and built in 1871. Its cruciform plan, comprising nave, transepts, central tower and chancel, is a beautifully articulated gothic form, as are the buttresses, pointed doorways, windows and side porch.

BATTERY WEED AND FORT TOMPKINS

SEE MILITARY HISTORY (FORT WADSWORTH)

Billiou-Stillwell-Perine House

1476 Richmond Road, Dongan Hills

This farmhouse, owned and maintained by the Staten Island Historical Society, was the residence of families of Belgian, British and French origin. The Billiou section was built circa 1662 by Pierre Billiou, a Belgian Walloon and leader of Staten Island's first permanent European colony. Its tall roof is visible in the middle, and its thick stone walls, steep roof, huge chimney and small windows suggest a medieval tradition from northern France. Nearest to Richmond Road stands the Stillwell section, built circa 1680 for Captain Thomas Stillwell, who married Billiou's daughter and attached his house to his father-in-law's. The Perine family occupied the entire house from 1764 to 1913, adding a clapboarded kitchen to the far left in 1790 and subsequently another kitchen to the far right.

The Ernest Flagg Estate was named for its builder, the famed architect Ernest Flagg, whose work includes the U.S. Naval Academy and the Singer Building, an early Manhattan skyscraper. *Courtesy of Staten Island Historical Society.*

Ernest Flagg Estate

209 Flagg Place, Todt Hill

Begun in 1897, the Ernest Flagg Estate included an entrance gate, gatehouse, gardener's house, greenhouse, water tower, stables and indoor and outdoor swimming pools. Its main house (named Stone Court) featured, on the land side, a front entrance through a walled courtyard in the French style. The ocean side is dominated by a two-story porch in the Dutch Caribbean style. Ernest Flagg (1857–1947), a renowned architect whose works include Manhattan's Singer Building, an early skyscraper (1899, demolished), and the U.S. Naval Academy (1908), Annapolis, had married Margaret Elizabeth Bonnell, a Staten Island native, and was attracted to Staten Island as a weekend retreat.

NEW YORK CITY FARM COLONY/SEAVIEW HOSPITAL HISTORIC DISTRICT

460 Brielle Avenue, Manor Heights

This historic district consists of two municipal institutions created to improve social and healthcare services. Farm Colony construction began in 1904 with striking Colonial Revival dormitories designed by Renwick, Aspinwall & Owen and was built of local rubble stone. By 1934, capacity was doubled with the completion of Colonial Revival brick structures designed by Charles B. Meyers. Architect Raymond F. Almirall planned and designed Seaview Hospital, founded in 1905 for the treatment of tuberculosis and located across Brielle Avenue from the Farm Colony. Later additions include Renwick, Aspinwall & Tucker's two groups of small open-air pavilions designed in 1917 for ambulatory patients.

FRANK LLOYD WRIGHT'S CRIMSON BEECH HOUSE

48 Manor Court, Lighthouse Hill

Named for the large beech tree on the property, this house was designed by Frank Lloyd Wright (1869–1959). Wright built it in 1959 for Mr. and Mrs. William Cass, who moved to Staten Island from Queens. The carport and natural wood finishes are indicative of Wright's Usonian design. Derived from the initial letters of the United States, these "Usonian Homes" referred to the ideal residences for the American family of average income, as Wright used the term. The house's horizontality is also a dramatic Wrightian characteristic.

THE JACQUES MARCHAIS MUSEUM OF TIBETAN ART

338 Lighthouse Avenue, Lighthouse Hill

The museum's fieldstone garden terraces afford spectacular views of the Atlantic Ocean. The complex was founded by Jacques Marchais (1887–1948), an Ohioan who moved to the Lighthouse Hill site in 1921 and soon began collecting Tibetan art. Her architectural inspiration came from Potala

The Jacques Marchais Museum of Tibetan Art, built between 1945 and 1947, resembles a Himalayan monastery. *Courtesy of the Tibetan Museum.*

of Lhasa, the Dalai Lama's historic residence. Like its model, it was originally approached by a long stairway from the bottom of the hill. Constructed between 1945 and 1947, the museum building resembles a Himalayan monastery, with its square shape and flat roof. High on its fieldstone walls, a series of trapezoidal-shaped windows lights the interior. The library, a horizontal single-story building, adjoins the museum.

HISTORIC RICHMOND TOWN

441 Clarke Avenue, Richmond

Richmond became the government center of Richmond County around 1710 when the first county jail and, shortly thereafter, the first courthouse were built. The Third County Courthouse (1837) presently stands at the top of the hill on Center Street. Its majestic columned portico expresses the importance of law and local county government. In the 1930s, the Staten Island Historical Society opened its museum in the former county clerk's and surrogate's office. In the 1960s, historic buildings from other nearby locations were moved to the village. Today, Historic Richmond Town is an

Voorlezer's House in Historic Richmond Town, built circa 1695, is one of the oldest, still-standing Dutch sites in New York City. *Photograph by William McMillen, 1986. Courtesy of Staten Island Historical Society.*

outdoor, living history museum of more than thirty historic buildings. Some of the best examples of early Dutch architecture left in New York City are found here, including the Voorlezer's House, the Christopher House, the Britton Cottage and the Treasure House.

CHURCH OF SAINT ANDREW

40 Old Mill Road, Richmond

The rough-cut stone walls of the Church of Saint Andrew (Episcopal) testify to the romantic period of American nineteenth-century architecture. The steep gables, battlements, roundheaded and bull's-eye windows recall English parish churches from the Norman period. George Mersereau, a Port Richmond builder and sash manufacturer, constructed the building in 1872 to replace a colonial building destroyed by fire. Part of the original end wall is incorporated into the present church. Burch Hall (1924) adjoining was designed by George's nephew, William H. Mersereau, a resident of New Dorp and a distinguished architect with projects from New York to Virginia.

HISTORIC RICHMOND TOWN'S DECKER FARM

SEE FOOD AND DRINK

VILLAGE GREENS

Arden Avenue, Arden Heights

Village Greens, which opened on August 2, 1970, is the earliest planned unit development on Staten Island. Developed by NY Loew's, in partnership with J.H. Snyder Co. of Los Angeles, and designed by Norman Jaffe (1932–1993), the thirty-five-acre site contains clustered town houses and open spaces with swimming pools, tennis courts, basketball courts, a baseball diamond and picnic areas. With a density of 12 houses per acre, the original plan included 2,025 town house units in nine clustered villages, not all of which were constructed.

FREDERICK LAW OLMSTED HOUSE

4515 Hylan Boulevard, Eltingville

Once the home of the designer of Manhattan's Central Park and of Brooklyn's Prospect Park, Frederick Law Olmsted, the original structure was built in the early eighteenth century. *Courtesy of Staten Island Museum.*

The stone portion of this structure was built in the early eighteenth century by Jacques Poillon, the county road commissioner. The relieving arches visible on the façade suggest that it may originally have been a barn. The frame second floor, attic and kitchen wing were added circa 1840. In 1847, Frederick Law Olmsted (1822–1903) purchased the farm and lived here until 1853. Olmsted grew fruit trees, experimented with farm techniques and landscape design and planted the cedars of Lebanon, ginkgo and walnut trees seen today in the front yard. He went on to design Central Park and Prospect Park and eventually became known as the founder of American landscape architecture. Olmsted remained active in Staten Island civic life and served with distinction on the Staten Island Improvement Commission of 1870, which created the nation's first regional plan for parks.

THE MEMORIAL CHURCH OF THE HUGUENOTS

5475 Amboy Road, Huguenot

In 1924, an international celebration of the 300th anniversary of the arrival of Huguenot (French) and Walloon (Belgian) refugees to New Netherlands was marked by the construction of this memorial church in Huguenot. *Courtesy of Staten Island Museum.*

This unusual building was dedicated in 1924 as the National Monument of the Huguenot–Walloon–New Netherlands 300th Anniversary of Religious Freedom. Designed by Ernest Flagg, it recalls vernacular Norman architecture of England and northwestern France. A concrete structure incorporating rubble stone quarried on Flagg's estate, it is today the Reformed Church of Huguenot Park. The assembly hall was designed by Staten Island architect James Whitford Jr. (1906–1976) and built in 1954, when the Huguenot Public Library was moved to the site. Once the smallest branch of the New York Public Library, it is now a private shop.

THE JOSEPH H. SEGUINE MANSION AND HISTORIC HOUSE MUSEUM

440 Seguine Avenue, Prince's Bay

In the nineteenth century, Prince's Bay held Staten Island's best-known oyster beds. Joseph H. Seguine, heir to a prosperous oyster business, built this Greek Revival home in 1838, overlooking a candle factory and the bay. With its six-columned temple front, the house testifies to Seguine's acumen as a businessman and status as a local aristocrat. After the Civil War, the house was sold by the Seguine family,

The Joseph H. Seguine House, a Greek Revival structure built in 1938 for farmer and oyster merchant Joseph H. Seguine, faces Prince's Bay. *Courtesy of Mary Bullock.*

subsequently repurchased by descendants in 1916 and sold again in 1981. The new owner, George Burke, a Tottenville interior decorator and Realtor, transferred the property to the City of New York with life tenancy.

WOODROW UNITED METHODIST CHURCH
SEE RELIGION

SANDY GROUND

Bloomingdale Road and Woodrow Road, Rossville

SEE ALSO BUSINESS AND THE ECONOMY

Sandy Ground houses largely resembled those of other Staten Island communities, and several large residences from the 1880s remain, like those of George Hunter, 575 Bloomingdale Road, and Isaac Harris, 444 Bloomingdale Road. The cottages at 565 and 569 Bloomingdale Road were built circa 1900 as rental units for oystermen. Opposite these cottages is the Rossville AME Zion Church, 584 Bloomingdale Road, built in 1897. The congregation began in 1850 and played a central role in the vibrant life of the community; it remains active today. The original church was built after 1854, on the Crabtree Avenue site where its cemetery now exists. In 1985, the burial ground was named a New York City landmark, and Sandy Ground is listed on the National Register of Historic Places.

THE CONFERENCE HOUSE
SEE CIVIC AND POLITICAL LIFE

CHARLES KREISCHER HOUSE

4500 Arthur Kill Road, Charleston

On a high bluff overlooking the village of Charleston, the Charles Kreischer House is a proud reminder of this once-prosperous German American family. Originally Kreischerville, the name of the village was changed to Charleston during World War I. In 1854, Balthazar Kreischer (1813–1886) established the Kreischer Brick Works on the shore of the Arthur Kill. In the 1880s, he built this house and its mirror-image twin for his sons, Charles C. and Edward B. Kreischer. Edward's house was demolished in the 1930s. The house is in the Stick style, featuring bold wooden braces under wide eaves, elaborate decoration at the gables, turned posts and ornate porch rails. With its turrets and tower, gables and balconies, it is also a version of the Queen Anne style.

TEMPLE EMANU-EL

984 Post Avenue, Port Richmond

SEE ALSO RELIGION

Completed in 1907, Temple Emanu-El displays aspects of neoclassical architecture popular at the time, with explicit references to Jewish heritage. Its architectural precedents rest in King Solomon's Temple in Jerusalem, with two giant columns, and the Great Synagogue in Warsaw, Poland, a temple-fronted building with a tall dome. Local architect Harry W. Pelcher designed Temple Emanu-El for a Conservative congregation, whose members had immigrated to America from Eastern Europe in the 1880s. Inside is a plaque commemorating the lives of six congregants who were killed in World War II.

McKIM, MEAD AND WHITE HOUSE

33 St. Austin's Place, West New Brighton

This attractive Colonial Revival house, and its mirror image across the street at No. 31, was designed by the celebrated architectural firm of McKim, Mead and White in 1893. The Colonial Revival style, sometimes called "modernized colonial," merged the Queen Anne style with eighteenth-century American Colonial features. Colonial references here include the shingle siding, six-over-six-paned windows, dormers and, beneath the eaves, dentil blocks and egg-and-dart trim. The house's large scale, its wraparound porch and extended front bay are more modern touches. The two houses were commissioned by the Henderson Estate Co., which laid out St. Austin's Place and other streets west of Sailors' Snug Harbor.

CORNELIUS CRUSER HOUSE

1262 Richmond Terrace, Livingston

This house of three laterally joined parts faces the Kill van Kull on a wide bend of Richmond Terrace west of Snug Harbor. The original section, on the right, was a one-room fieldstone house built in 1722 for Cornelius Van Santvoord, minister of the Dutch Reformed Church in Port Richmond. Cornelius Cruser, a farmer and son of the voorlezer of the Dutch Church, added the three-bay central section, made of rough-cut stone and now clad with scalloped shingles, in 1770. Daniel Pelton Sr., a published poet and abolitionist, moved to the island from Manhattan in 1835 and built the brick section on the left the following year. During the American Revolution, the house was the headquarters for General Cortlandt Skinner of the Loyalist New Jersey Volunteers. It is believed that Prince William Henry, the future King William IV of England, occasionally visited General Skinner at the house, and that British spy major John André spent time here as well.

SAILORS' SNUG HARBOR

1000 Richmond Terrace, New Brighton

SEE ALSO EDUCATION AND HEALTH, THE ARTS AND ENVIRONMENT

From 1831 to 1918, when the buildings of Sailors' Snug Harbor were constructed, Americans looked to European architecture for inspiration. The iron fence and the middle three buildings of the row fronting Richmond Terrace, as well as the obelisk and pedestal, are of the early nineteenth-century Greek Revival style. The mid-nineteenth-century buildings, including the dining hall, chapel and four later dormitories, reflect the eclecticism of the Italianate style. The third major group of buildings, including the Music Hall, the Randall Memorial Church (demolished 1953) and the Recreation Hall, date to the Gilded Age (1876–1917). They appropriated Renaissance motifs with an American emphasis.

Tysen-Neville House

806 Richmond Terrace, New Brighton

This farmhouse on the Kill van Kull is the largest Staten Island residence to survive from the late eighteenth century. It was built for Richard Housman shortly after he acquired the farm in 1782. The front wall, now painted white, is composed of cut sandstone in a checkerboard pattern. Prominent nineteenth-century residents included civil court judge and U.S. congressman Jacob Tysen and John I. Neville, a retired naval officer, both men having married daughters of the home's owners. In 1882, the house became the Knickerbocker Hotel, which was nicknamed "The Old Stone Jug," a tavern for Sailors' Snug Harbor residents.

The Tysen-Neville House is the largest still-standing residence on Staten Island from the late eighteenth century. By the late nineteenth century, the house was being used as a hotel and tavern. *Photograph by Percy Sperr, 1932. Courtesy of Staten Island Historical Society.*

Chapter 11

MILITARY HISTORY

Phillip Papas

Contributors: Lee Covino, Jason Wickersty and Joseph M. Margiotta

There are only two things I want to accomplish in this war. The first is, in the performance of my duty, to make the maximum contribution to the winning of the war; and secondly, to reach home alive.
—*Staten Islander John Millard in 1944*

For generations, Staten Islanders have answered their country's call to service in wartime or have done their part on the homefront. The heroism and sacrifices of island veterans are commemorated in monuments, memorials and parks across the island. Five Staten Islanders received the Congressional Medal of Honor: Lieutenant Theodore W. Greig and Sergeant Joseph Keele (Civil War), Private Joseph F. Merrell Jr. (World War II), Hospital Corpsman Third Class Edward C. Benfold (Korean War) and Lieutenant Father Vincent R. Capodanno (Vietnam War).

During the American Revolution, the British military occupied Staten Island. Most Staten Islanders were Loyalists, but some, like the Mersereau family of Port Richmond, fought for American independence. Following the War of 1812, America developed coastal defenses that included Fort Wadsworth. In the early twentieth century, coastal defense evolved from fortifications to airfields like Miller Field.

During the Civil War (1861–1865), Union army training camps were located on Staten Island. In July 1863, the island experienced a spillover of violence from the New York City Draft Riots. Staten Island was also home to

Colonel Robert G. Shaw, who commanded the Fifty-fourth Massachusetts, an African American regiment.

Staten Islanders fought bravely in the two world wars. They also worked in shipyards, munitions and aircraft factories, hospitals and civil defense jobs. They bought Liberty Bonds, planted victory gardens, collected scrap metal and volunteered for the Red Cross or the USO. Mary Otis Gay Wilcox, Adelaide Irving, Ethel Fowler, Jessie Vanderbilt Simons and the photographer Alice Austen were important female Staten Islanders active in the Red Cross during the world wars. Hundreds of thousands of service personnel and tons of supplies departed from the Stapleton piers (Staten Island Terminal) for combat theaters overseas. The Manhattan Project stored uranium for the atomic bomb near the Bayonne Bridge.

Staten Island's Korean War (1950–1953) veterans are proud of their service in America's "Forgotten War" because, as one of them put it, "we stopped communism." The eighty-four Staten Islanders who were killed in the Vietnam War (1961–1975) was the highest per-capita toll of any American community. Many Staten Islanders have served in Iraq and Afghanistan since the terrorist attacks of September 11, 2001. Staten Island's veterans have always been active in the community, participating in parades and civic celebrations and educating schoolchildren on the importance of defending cherished liberties.

Paulo Park Veterans Memorial and Skirmish at St. Andrew's Church, Borough Hall Mural

1776 Stuyvesant Place, St. George

At the foot of the Richmond Terrace flagpole in Judge Frank Paulo Memorial Park, a memorial honoring all Staten Island veterans was completed in 1991. Its text reads: "To the Veterans of Staten Island Who Have Served in Times of War and Peace We Give Thanks to God and Remember Those Men and Women Especially Those Who Have Made the Ultimate Sacrifice and Those Who Remain Unaccounted for in the Pursuit of Freedom." A WPA mural inside Borough Hall depicts the skirmish at St. Andrew's Church in Richmond during the October 1776 raid of British-occupied Staten Island by Continental forces commanded by General Hugh Mercer.

After the Civil War, military parades for Decoration Day (now Memorial Day) and Armistice Day (now Veterans Day) became common on Staten Island. In this photo, members of the Fifty-first Cavalry Brigade of the New York State National Guard, based at the Armory on Manor Road, march in one such parade along Richmond Terrace. *Courtesy of Staten Island Historical Society.*

MAJOR CLARENCE T. BARRETT MEMORIAL

Borough Place Triangle, St. George

Erected in 1915 and designed by Sherry Edmundson Fry, this monument was given to New York City by Anna Hutchings Barrett and was dedicated to her husband, Major Clarence T. Barrett of the 175th New York Volunteer Regiment in the Civil War. After the war, Barrett became a renowned landscape architect and civil engineer and served as police commissioner of Staten Island and superintendent of the poor. The Staten Island Zoo is located on the former Barrett estate.

FORT HILL PARK/FORT KNYPHAUSEN

Fort Hill Circle, St. George

This was one of several redoubts (small forts) built by the British and their Hessian and Loyalist allies on Staten Island during the American Revolution. The redoubt that was located here, known as Fort Knyphausen, was named for Hessian general Wilhelm von Knyphausen. The Hessians came mainly from the German principalities of Hesse-Cassel and Brunswick. Britain's King George III hired them to supplement his military forces in America.

MERCHANT MARINERS MEMORIAL

Richmond Terrace and the Staten Island Ferry Viaduct, St. George

During World War II, the U.S. Merchant Marine provided a crucial link between the production of war material at home and American fighting forces around the world. The Merchant Mariners Memorial was dedicated in May 1996.

WATERING PLACE: AFRICAN AMERICAN LOYALISTS

Victory Boulevard and Bay Street, Tompkinsville

Choosing sides in the American Revolution was difficult for many Americans. On Staten Island, the great majority were Loyalist. For enslaved African Americans, personal liberty mattered most. The British actively recruited slaves belonging to Patriot masters, promising them freedom. At this site, the British army established its main encampment on Staten Island in 1776. The British presence on the island attracted Loyalist refugees, many of them African Americans escaping slavery. African American Loyalists lived in segregated quarters, worked as manual laborers and nurses or joined Black Loyalist regiments. The percentage of African Americans on Staten Island increased to nearly 25 percent during the American Revolution. After the war, some of these refugees settled in Nova Scotia, Canada, and later helped to establish the West African nation of Sierra Leone. This site had previously been used as a staging area for British troops, preparing for an expedition against the French sugar island of Martinique in 1761 during the French and Indian War (1754–1763), and was visited by the commander in chief of British Forces in North America, General Jeffrey Amherst.

THE HIKER MONUMENT

Tompkinsville Park, Tompkinsville

Dedicated in 1916, this monument honors the 150 Staten Islanders who served in the Spanish-American War. Designed by sculptor Allen G. Newman, it is one of several Newman Hikers in the country. The lone Staten Islander killed in the war was Private Joseph S. Decker of Tottenville.

HOME PORT (NAVAL STATION NEW YORK)

355 Front Street, Stapleton

In 1983, the U.S. Navy selected this site as the home port for a squadron headed by the battleship USS *Iowa*. The squadron also included the guided missile cruiser USS *Normandy*. The home port plan sparked controversy when it was believed that tomahawk missiles aboard the *Iowa* and the *Normandy* might carry nuclear warheads. Years of debate followed, stalling the planned base. By 1993, cutbacks in military spending and the collapse of the Soviet Union led the U.S. Navy to close the home port. The annual Fleet Week brings navy and coast guard ships to the piers.

MATTHEW J. BUONO MONUMENT

Edgewater Street, Rosebank

This monument, dedicated in 2001, honors the residents of the Rosebank area who died in World Wars I and II and the Korean and Vietnam Wars. It is named for Matthew J. Buono of Rosebank, who was killed during the Vietnam War.

FORT WADSWORTH

New York Avenue, Fort Wadsworth

Strategically located at the entrance to the Narrows, this site dates back to the colonial period in military importance. In June 1776, Continental forces built the Flagstaff Fort here, which was later captured by the British. After the War of 1812, Forts Richmond and Tompkins were constructed for coastal defense. They were replaced with Battery Weed, completed in 1861, and a rebuilt Fort Tompkins in 1876. Battery Weed, a trapezoid at the water's edge, was designed by Joseph G. Totten, the U.S. Army's chief engineer. It was named after General Stephen Weed, killed at the Battle of Gettysburg. Atop a steep bluff, Fort Tompkins is a pentagonal structure containing gun emplacements and soldiers' living quarters. It was named for Daniel D. Tompkins (1774–1825), governor of New York during the

Built after the War of 1812 for coastal defense, Fort Wadsworth guarded the entrance to the Narrows. It was named in honor of Union army general James S. Wadsworth. *Photograph by Alice Austen, 1893. Courtesy of Staten Island Historical Society.*

This monument on the grounds of Fort Wadsworth is dedicated to Lieutenant Vincent R. Capodanno, a Catholic priest who posthumously received the Congressional Medal of Honor for heroism during the Vietnam War. *Courtesy of Lee Covino.*

War of 1812 and vice president of the United States under James Monroe. The entire facility was named in honor of Union army general James S. Wadsworth, who was killed at the Battle of the Wilderness in 1864. Turned over to the Department of the Interior in 1995, it opened to the public as part of Gateway National Recreation Area two years later. On its grounds are monuments to Congressional Medal of Honor recipient, priest and U.S. Navy chaplain lieutenant Vincent R. Capodanno and to the "Four Chaplains" of the United States Army Transport (USAT) *Dorchester*, as well as the Staten Island War Dog Memorial.

THE FATHER VINCENT R. CAPODANNO MEMORIAL AND THE FREEDOM CIRCLE

FDR Boardwalk, South Beach

The Father Vincent R. Capodanno Memorial, dedicated in July 1976, commemorates the life of U.S. Navy chaplain lieutenant Vincent R. Capodanno, a South Beach resident and Catholic priest, who was posthumously awarded the Congressional Medal of Honor for heroism during the Vietnam War. At the southern end of FDR Boardwalk is Freedom Circle, a monument featuring six flags from important moments in American history. Opened in 2005, it honors the service and sacrifice of the United States armed forces.

MIDLAND BEACH VETERANS MEMORIAL

Father Capodanno Boulevard, Midland Beach

This memorial, which was erected in 2004, is dedicated to the twelve residents of the Midland Beach area who served and died in World Wars I and II, the Korean War and the Vietnam War.

MILLER FIELD

600 New Dorp Lane, New Dorp

This site was formerly the property of Cornelius Vanderbilt. During the Civil War, it was home to Camp Vanderbilt, a military training ground.

In the early twentieth century, the Vanderbilt family built the Clubhouse Grounds Trotting Course. In 1919, the federal government purchased the property from the Vanderbilt family in order to establish the Air Coast Defense Station at New Dorp. In January 1920, it was renamed for Captain James E. Miller, the first American aviator killed in action for the United States in World War I. In 1928, Admiral Richard E. Byrd tested his new plane here, the Floyd Bennett, prior to his first expedition to Antarctica. During World War II, Miller Field had warehouses that were used to store military equipment, temporary housing facilities for soldiers, a watchtower and antiaircraft guns. It had the last grass runway in New York City and remained an active airfield until its deactivation by the U.S. Army in 1969. It subsequently became part of the National Park Service's Gateway National Recreation Area, and in 1999, it was designated as World War Veterans Park at Miller Field. Its facilities for soccer, football, baseball, softball, lacrosse and cricket are now used by 750,000 athletes, fans and visitors annually.

New Dorp World War II Memorial

New Dorp Lane and Ninth Street, New Dorp

Erected in September 1947, this large granite memorial is dedicated to the residents of New Dorp who served in World War II. The ceremonies accompanying its unveiling included a parade and speeches by prominent local officials and veterans.

New Dorp Memorial Park

Richmond Road and New Dorp Lane, New Dorp

Here once stood the Rose and Crown Tavern, a popular meeting place for British general William Howe and his staff in 1776. It was here that Howe first read a copy of the Declaration of Independence. The tavern was demolished in 1854. Also at this site is the New Dorp World War I Memorial, honoring the sixty-six residents of New Dorp who served in the Great War.

COLONEL ROBERT G. SHAW MEMORIAL

Moravian Cemetery, New Dorp

This memorial honors Colonel Robert G. Shaw, who during the Civil War commanded the Fifty-fourth Massachusetts Volunteer Infantry, an African American regiment. Born in Boston, Shaw migrated to Staten Island with his family, settling in Livingston. His parents, Francis George and Sarah Blake Sturgis Shaw, were prominent abolitionists. On July 18, 1863, Shaw led the Fifty-fourth in an ill-fated assault on Confederate Fort Wagner in Charleston Harbor, South Carolina. He was killed during the assault and buried with his men in a mass grave near the fort. The heroism of Colonel Shaw and his men was depicted in the 1989 film *Glory*.

MEMORIAL GARDEN AT POUCH CAMP

Manor Road, Manor Heights

Situated in William H. Pouch Camp, the memorial garden features several monuments and memorials that were dedicated between 2004 and 2009: the Purple Heart Memorial, the KIA (Killed in Action) Memorial, the Catholic War Veterans Memorial, the Jewish War Veterans Monument, the United Staten Island Veterans Organization Monument, the Anzio Beachhead Memorial, the Medical Monument, the Disabled Veterans Monument, the War Dogs Monument and the Armed Forces Flags.

EGBERTVILLE WORLD WAR I MEMORIAL

Richmond Road and Rockland Avenue, Egbertville

This memorial honors the forty-one residents of Egbertville who served in World War I. It consists of a granite stele with a bronze eagle and plaque.

LOOKOUT PLACE AT RICHMOND HILL

Richmond Hill Road, New Springville (Former Site)

An earthen redoubt once existed at this site. Constructed in 1776 by British Regulars, it overlooked the village of Richmond. This small fort housed British Regulars as well as Loyalist and Hessian troops. American prisoners were also held here.

GREAT KILLS VETERANS MEMORIAL

Great Kills Train Station, Great Kills

This memorial is dedicated to those Staten Islanders who have served in the U.S. armed forces from the American Revolution to the conflicts in Iraq and Afghanistan. It takes the form of five carved black granite slabs, each one representing a service branch of the U.S. military. Dedicated in 2001, the memorial was designed in collaboration with the Department of Defense. The Great Kills Memorial Day Parade, which has been held annually since 1995, ceremonially ends at the memorial.

BATTLE OF THE BULGE MEMORIAL

Wolfe's Pond Park, Huguenot

The Battle of the Bulge, which began on December 16, 1944, in Europe's Ardennes Forest, was the bloodiest battle that American forces experienced in World War II. This memorial, completed in 2001, honors those who participated in the battle. Citizens of Belgium and Luxembourg donated seven of its cobblestone rings. The monument features two black granite slabs that symbolize the heroism of the Americans and their allies during the battle.

PLEASANT PLAINS WORLD WAR I MEMORIAL

Pleasant Plains Plaza, Pleasant Plains

This memorial, once known as the Soldiers and Sailors Monument or the Pleasant Plains War Monument, was created by Tottenville sculptor George T. Brewster and erected on June 9, 1923. It commemorates the thirteen South Shore residents who died in World War I. The Russell Pavilion in Conference House Park, Tottenville,

Erected in June 1923, this monument was originally known as the Soldiers and Sailors Monument, or the Pleasant Plains War Monument. It honors the lives of the thirteen South Shore residents who died in World War I. *Courtesy of Staten Island Historical Society.*

was named for one of them, Almer G. Russell. The statue of a woman holding a sword and palm frond above her head as an eagle sits at her feet represents Brewster's interpretation of the ideals of victory and peace. The original statue, which was damaged several times from automobile accidents, was removed for repairs in 1970. It mysteriously disappeared from storage in 1975, and a replica was installed in 1996. The memorial was rededicated in June 1997.

CONFERENCE HOUSE (BILLOPP HOUSE)
SEE CIVIC AND POLITICAL LIFE

TRAVIS WORLD WAR I AND WORLD WAR II MEMORIALS

Victory Boulevard and Cannon Avenue, Victory Boulevard and Shelly Avenue, Travis

The Travis World War I Memorial honors the seventy-five residents of Travis who fought in World War I, especially the nine who were killed in action. The flat stone monument features a relief depicting an American Doughboy running out of his trenches and the words "America Over the Top" inscribed above him. A Revolutionary War–era cannon stands in front. The World War II Memorial lists the names of those residents of Travis killed in the war. Travis is famous for its annual Fourth of July parade, which in 2010 celebrated its centennial.

HALLORAN GENERAL HOSPITAL

College of Staten Island (CUNY), Willowbrook

This was the largest army hospital in America when it opened in October 1942. Named for Colonel Paul Stacey Halloran of the U.S. Medical Corps, Halloran was a basic training site for the Army Nurse Corps. On its staff were Japanese Americans and African Americans, including Ruth Wallace, who was the first commissioned dietician of color in the U.S. Army. Its grounds had a POW camp that held over six hundred German prisoners, many of them working in the hospital. Celebrities, such as the "Singing Cowboy" Roy Rogers, often entertained the patients. Halloran closed as a military hospital in 1947 and operated as a veterans' hospital until 1951. Originally built in 1938 by New York state as a facility for mentally handicapped children, the site was later occupied by the Willowbrook State School until 1987.

EGBERT TRIANGLE AND MEMORIAL

Port Richmond Avenue, Port Richmond

When Egbert Triangle was built in 1929, it was known as Egbert Square. It was named for Seaman Second Class Arthur S. Egbert of Graniteville, who died in 1918 when the USS *President Lincoln* was sunk by a German submarine. The monument was dedicated to Egbert and the other residents of Graniteville, as well as those from Port Richmond, who died in World War I. It was renamed Egbert Triangle in 1998.

PATRIOTS PARK

340 Walker Street, Elm Park

Dedicated in 2005, Patriots Park honors all of Staten Island's war dead from the Civil War to the conflicts in Iran and Afghanistan. Their names are inscribed on several large granite monuments. Patriots Park includes a monument to the victims of 9/11 and was the site of the first Vietnam Veterans Memorial on Staten Island in the late 1960s.

MANHATTAN PROJECT STORAGE SITE

Richmond Terrace near the Bayonne Bridge, Port Richmond

During World War II, the federal government stored more than four thousand drums of uranium from the Belgian Congo in a warehouse at this site. The uranium was used for the secret scientific research effort known as the Manhattan Project, which developed the atomic bomb. The warehouse was torn down in 1976.

REFORMED CHURCH OF STATEN ISLAND

SEE RELIGION

VETERANS PARK

Park Avenue and Bennett Street, Port Richmond

Dating to 1838, Staten Island's oldest public park became the center of an annual Flag Day parade after 1911. In 1943, more than three thousand spectators attended the dedication of its flagpole by Gold Star Mother Mary Kitchner. In the park is a monument erected by the Daughters of the American Revolution to commemorate the August 22, 1777 raid of British-occupied Staten Island by Continental forces under General John Sullivan. The monument emphasizes the valor of General William Smallwood's troops during the raid. The park was renamed Veterans Park in 1949 as a tribute to American veterans.

JEWISH WORLD WAR II MEMORIAL AT TEMPLE EMANU-EL

SEE ARCHITECTURE

CAMP McCLELLAN, CIVIL WAR TRAINING CAMP

Between Castleton Avenue and Richmond Terrace, West Brighton (Former Site)

This was one of several Union army training camps on Staten Island during the Civil War. It operated from August to November 1861 and was named for Union army commander general George B. McClellan. Other training camps included Camps Decker, Ward and Low in the Port Richmond/Elm Park area; Camps Arthur and Washington in Tompkinsville; Camps Herndon and Morrison in Stapleton; Camp Leslie in the Clifton/Rosebank area; Camp Scott near Old Town; Camps Lafayette, Sprague, Vanderbilt (now Miller Field) and Yates in the New

Dorp/New Dorp Beach area; and Forts Richmond and Tompkins in Fort Wadsworth. There was also a small encampment at Cedar Grove Beach and a Camp Ironsides of unknown location.

CORNELIUS CRUSER HOUSE
SEE ARCHITECTURE

STATEN ISLAND ARMORY AND THE STATEN ISLAND VIETNAM VETERANS MEMORIAL

321 Manor Road, Castleton Corners

Built in 1926 to resemble a Norman castle, the Staten Island Armory was the headquarters for the 51st Cavalry Brigade of the New York State National Guard until 1941. It also housed the 1st Battalion, 101st Cavalry Division of the New York State National Guard, until 2006. It was one of four active armories in New York City when it was designated a landmark by the city's Landmarks Preservation Commission in 2010. Established in 1988 and maintained by the Thomas J. Tori Post, Chapter 421, of the Vietnam Veterans of America, the Staten Island Vietnam Veterans Memorial is

Built in 1926, the Staten Island Armory was originally the headquarters for the Fifty-first Cavalry Brigade of the New York State National Guard until 1941. It was one of four active armories in New York City when it was designated a landmark by the city in 2010. *Photograph by Herbert A. Flamm. Courtesy of Staten Island Historical Society.*

Established in 1988, the Staten Island Vietnam Veterans Memorial, at the corner of Manor Road and Martling Avenue, honors the lives of the eighty-four Staten Islanders who were killed in action in the Vietnam War and those still missing in action. *Courtesy of College of Staten Island, CUNY.*

dedicated to the eighty-four Staten Islanders who were killed in the Vietnam War and to those who are still missing in action.

World War II Veterans Memorial Ice Skating Rink and the Private Joseph F. Merrell Jr. Monument

1321 Victory Boulevard, West New Brighton

See also Environment and Sports

The World War II Veterans Memorial Ice Skating Rink (formerly the War Memorial Ice Skating Rink) opened in 1987 in Clove Lakes Park. Adjacent to the rink is the Private Joseph F. Merrell Jr. Monument. This monument, erected in 1993, honors the posthumous awardee of the Congressional Medal of Honor for his heroism during World War II.

Korean War Veterans Memorial

Ocean Terrace and Milford Drive, Sunnyside

Dedicated in 1996, this memorial honors those Staten Islanders who served in the Korean War (1950–1953). The names of the thirty-five Staten Islanders killed in the war are inscribed on the memorial. There are also three flagpoles dedicated to the Korean War veterans of Staten Island and to a civilian liaison between the veterans and the Staten Island Korean community.

CONCORD WORLD WAR II MEMORIAL

Targee Street and Clove Road, Concord

This memorial, which was erected in 1947, honors those Staten Islanders who were killed in World War II, sixteen of them from Concord. It also lists President Franklin D. Roosevelt as a casualty of the war. The memorial was rededicated in 1969.

POW/MIA MEMORIAL PARK

Narrows Road North and Targee Street, Concord

This site, once an illegal truck stop, was transformed in 1998 into a memorial park honoring Americans who were held as prisoners of war and those who are still missing in action. It contains a small stone monument and a flagpole, which flies the American flag and the official POW/MIA flag. The memorial park was made possible through the efforts of the owners of the My Deli grocery store, Hamim and Doreen Syed, and the DeKalb Street Merchants Association.

FOX HILLS HOSPITAL/ U.S. DEBARKATION HOSPITAL

Vanderbilt Avenue, Clifton (Former Site)

When the Fox Hills Hospital was opened in 1918 to serve wounded veterans of World War I, it was the largest army hospital in the world. It remained open until 1922, when concerns over deplorable conditions led to its closure. During World War II, the U.S. Army reopened the hospital after establishing a training post and a

The Fox Hills Hospital was opened in 1918 to serve wounded veterans of World War I. When it opened, it was the largest army hospital in the world. This photo of the hospital's interior shows several wounded veterans, as well as several of the Red Cross nurses who tended to them. *Courtesy of Staten Island Historical Society.*

camp for Italian and German POWs along nearby Vanderbilt Avenue. After the war, the hospital was converted into temporary housing for returning veterans. It closed in the early 1950s.

HERO PARK

Victory Boulevard and Louis Street, Grymes Hill

This site honors the 144 Staten Islanders who died in World War I and their mothers. The land was donated to New York City by local philanthropists Dr. Louis and Berta Dreyfus in 1920. Its main features are the evergreen trees that are dedicated to the deceased servicemen and the large granite boulder memorial known popularly as Sugar Loaf Rock.

Students from I.S. 49, the Berta Dreyfus School, pay homage to the 144 veterans listed on the Hero Park memorial plaque erected by the school's namesake. Principal Linda Hill, inspired by si350, organized a month of interdisciplinary learning about local history in collaboration with Wagner College professors Stephen Preskill and Lori R. Weintrob, Peggy Travers of the College of Staten Island GEAR-UP, Lee Covino (Office of the Borough President Veterans Affairs), borough historian Thomas Matteo and the NYC Parks Department. Pictured are (from left): Richard Candia (I.S. 49 teacher), Covino, Matteo, Hill, Steven Warcholak (I.S. 49 teacher) and I.S. 49 students. *Courtesy of Linda Hill.*

Chapter 12

RELIGION

Patricia M. Salmon

Contributors: Cheryl Bontales, Linda Hauck,
Hashem El-Meligy, Christopher Mulé,
Lynn Rogers and Lori R. Weintrob

The religious connections found on Staten Island give insight into the transformation of the borough, the city of New York and the United States. The faith expressed began with the original residents of Staten Island: the Lenape.

After the arrival of Europeans, a church was established at what is now called Arthur Kill Road and Richmond Avenue in Greenridge. Organized in 1683, it was known as the French Church. Initially, the congregation consisted of French Huguenots, Dutch and Anglican worshippers, but in 1696, the Dutch departed to commence a church of their own. Soon the Anglicans left for this very same reason.

In subsequent years, members of the African Methodist Episcopal, Moravian, Methodist, Unitarian, Lutheran, Roman Catholic, Presbyterian, Baptist, Jewish, Greek Orthodox and Magyar Reformed religions erected houses of worship. Today, Buddhism, Islam, Hinduism, Coptic Orthodox, Pentecostal and numerous other religions are also practiced on Staten Island.

The beliefs of islanders are further documented at a former slave cemetery, Mount Manresa, the Mount Carmel Grotto and the oldest funeral home in New York City, the Bedell-Pizzo Funeral Home. The varied and intricate web of religions offers a trail that is not only an invitation to discover faith and history but one that also allows for the investigation of ethnicity, diversity, culture and, in some cases, tolerance and intolerance.

SAINT PETER'S ROMAN CATHOLIC CHURCH

53 Saint Mark's Place, St. George

In April 1839, Roman Catholic Mass was celebrated in a gun factory on Lafayette Avenue in New Brighton. This was the humble start of both Saint Peter's and the Catholic Church on Staten Island. The growing flock was able to dedicate a real church five years later. The parish included the quarantine station at Tompkinsville; thus, the priests of Saint Peter's tended to the ailing Irish and German Catholic immigrants. After a fire, the current building was dedicated in 1903. In 1853, the Sisters of Charity began a parish school. Around 1850, a cemetery was established on Clove Road in West New Brighton. Monsignor James Dorney was named pastor of Saint Peter's in 1986. He has been regional vicar since 1998.

QUARANTINE CEMETERIES

Central Avenue and Hyatt Street, St. George; Silver Lake Golf Course, 915 Victory Boulevard, Silver Lake; and Wolfe's Pond Park, Cornelia Street, Prince's Bay

Long before Ellis Island was established, a quarantine station was opened at Tompkinsville. Beginning in 1799, immigrants with such communicable diseases as tuberculosis, yellow fever, typhoid and smallpox were isolated at the facility. It reached from the south side of the Ferry Terminal, up Hyatt Street and southward to Victory Boulevard. Oftentimes these diseases spread to the surrounding community. Attempts were made to relocate the quarantine, but when they failed, local residents burned the facility down in 1858. In order to accommodate the quarantine dead, cemeteries were established at this site, and also at Silver Lake and Prince's Bay.

TRINITY EVANGELICAL LUTHERAN CHURCH

309 Saint Paul's Avenue, Stapleton

Trinity was founded in 1856 by a group of German immigrants. The present gothic structure dates to 1913. The large stained-glass windows in the sanctuary were made in Munich, Germany, by the Mayer Company. The Reverend Dr. Frederic Sutter, pastor from 1907 to 1964, brought his alma mater, Wagner College, to Staten Island in 1918. He was succeeded by his son, the Reverend Dr. Carl Sutter, who created Trinity Lutheran School in 1964, currently serving over two hundred youth annually. The Reverend Dr. Thomas F. Mugavero and then Reverend Richard F. Michaels have led the congregation as it has diversified. Since 1987, it has sponsored a food pantry and soup kitchen on Saturdays.

STAPLETON UNITED AME CHURCH

49 Tompkins Avenue, Stapleton

The Stapleton United American Methodist Episcopal Church dates back to at least 1839 and perhaps as early as 1798. Bishop Isaac Barney was an important pastor from 1838 to 1843, and both he and his wife are interred on church property. Construction on the current church building began in 1922. Historically, the Stapleton church has provided food to the needy through both a soup kitchen and a food pantry. One of Staten Island's most well-known volunteers, Mamie Daniels, has long coordinated these important programs.

MASJID AL-NOOR/MUSLIM MAJLIS OF STATEN ISLAND

104 Rhine Avenue, Concord

In the 1960s, six families from Pakistan began meeting for prayer and social gatherings in their Staten Island homes. By 1985, they established Masjid Al-Noor, or Muslim Majlis of Staten Island. The trustees and imam are Pakistani, but like most mosques, it serves a wide variety of ethnicities. Four other mosques also serve the borough, including over one thousand families

The first mosque on Staten Island, the Masjid Al-Noor Mosque, was founded over twenty-five years ago. *Courtesy of Hesham El-Meligy.*

at Noor-Al Islam Center, 3075 Richmond Terrace, and over two thousand families at the Albanian Islamic Cultural Center, 307 Victory Boulevard.

OUR LADY OF MOUNT CARMEL GROTTO

36 Amity Street, Rosebank

An example of ethnic religious folk art, the Shrine of Our Lady of Mount Carmel was established to honor the Virgin Mary. It was initially constructed in 1937 by Vito Russo, with assistance from Thomas Tedesco. Simple artifacts, such as seashells, pebbles, rocks, glass, bicycle reflectors and statues, adorn the structure. Additional arches were added as the years unfolded. It is the largest indigenous Roman Catholic shrine and considered one of the finest examples of that art form in the city. Since 1903, the shrine has been highlighted during the annual Our Lady of Mount Carmel Society feast on July 16. In 2000, this site was added to the National Register of Historic Places.

MOUNT MANRESA

239 Fingerboard Road, Fort Wadsworth

In 1911, Father Terence J. Shealy selected the former Fox Hill Villa estate of Louis Meyer as the site for the first lay retreat in the United States. Built by Samuel Bowne in about 1852, Meyer purchased the estate in 1861. Mount Manresa is for individuals of any denomination who are seeking respite, relaxation or spiritual enhancement. A water tower, the Sacred Heart Grotto, the Sacred Heart Chapel, gardens and numerous structures lend to the retreat experience.

NEW DORP MORAVIAN CHURCH AND CEMETERY

2005 Richmond Road, New Dorp

The first Moravian church on Staten Island was dedicated in 1763, and the present Greek Revival building was consecrated in 1845. The building

The New Dorp
Moravian Church
was dedicated in
1763 and was the first
church of this faith on
Staten Island. Here
is a postcard of the
Moravian church,
New Dorp, circa
1905. *Gift of William
T. Davis, Staten Island
Museum.*

is used today by the trustees of the United Brethren's Church on Staten
Island, comprised of the Moravian congregations of New Dorp, Great Kills
and Castleton Hill. The Moravian Cemetery was incorporated in 1842. The
original tract of land was once owned by Thomas Dongan, a seventeenth-
century colonial governor of New York.

Vanderbilt Mausoleum and Cemetery

West of Moravian Cemetery, New Dorp (Private, No Public Access)

To design the Vanderbilt Mausoleum and Cemetery, William H. Vanderbilt
brought in the foremost designers of the 1880s, Richard Morris Hunt and
Frederick Law Olmsted. Hunt designed the mausoleum, while Olmsted
developed the landscape plan. Direct male descendants of "Commodore"

The Vanderbilt Mausoleum
was designed by the
renowned designer Richard
Hunt Morris. Direct
male descendants of
nineteenth-century tycoon
and native Staten Islander
"Commodore" Cornelius
Vanderbilt and their wives
can be interred within
it. *Courtesy of Staten Island
Museum.*

Cornelius Vanderbilt, and their wives, can be interred in the tomb's niches. Unmarried daughters of descendants are buried in the floor. The surrounding land is the final resting place for other Vanderbilt family relatives. Twenty-two acres in size, the Vanderbilt Cemetery is a separate entity from Moravian Cemetery.

CHURCH OF SAINT ANDREW

40 Old Mill Road, Richmond

Formally organized in the early eighteenth century, the Church of Saint Andrew was the first Anglican church on Staten Island. *Courtesy of Staten Island Museum.*

The Church of Saint Andrew (Episcopal) was formally organized soon after the arrival of the Reverend Aeneas Mackenzie in 1708. In 1711, William and Mary Tillyer donated land for a church and cemetery. During the Revolution it was used by the British as a hospital. Members of the Latourette, Perine, Simonson, Guyon, Poillon, Seguine, Van Duzer and Van Pelt families are a small sampling of the surnames found at this burial ground. The cemetery contains the oldest "documented" burial on Staten Island, the brownstone headstone of Ruth Dongan, who was interred in 1733.

"THE FRENCH CHURCH"

Arthur Kill Road between Gifford's Lane and Richmond Avenue, Greenridge (Built Over)

The first documented place of worship on Staten Island was founded here in 1683. French Huguenots, Belgian Walloons, Dutch, English, slaves and Native Americans composed the congregation. Members of the Dutch Reform and Anglican churches also utilized this church since their own affiliations lacked local houses of worship. As many as two hundred headstones once stood at the burial ground, but only a few were recognizable by 1850. By 1734, the majority of worshippers had become permanent members of the Church of Saint Andrew. Others had previously joined the Dutch Reformed Church.

Coptic Orthodox Church of Archangel Michael and Saint Mena

4095 Amboy Road, Great Kills

The Staten Island Coptic community is composed of Egyptian Christians and their descendants, as well as those of African, Spanish and Russian backgrounds. Founded in AD 41, the Christian church in Egypt is believed to include direct descendants of the pharaohs. An annual hymn competition has been held since 1994. When the new Coptic Orthodox church was opened in 2002, a Coptic nun came from Egypt to paint the icons. The annual Egyptian festival, formerly held in the mid-1980s at the Staten Island Armory in Castleton Corners, draws hundreds to enjoy Middle Eastern food, artworks and leather imports.

Dorothy Day Grave Site

Cemetery of the Resurrection, 361 Sharrott Avenue, Pleasant Plains

Born in Brooklyn, Dorothy Day and Peter Maurin began the Catholic Worker movement with publication of the *Catholic Worker* in 1933. It is still printed today. They also began feeding, clothing and housing the poor. Day lived on Staten Island at various times during her life; one location was the Annadale beach colony known as Spanish Camp. While living on Staten Island in 1927, she converted to Catholicism. On November 29, 1980, Day passed away and was buried at the Cemetery of the Resurrection. Dorothy Day is currently being considered for sainthood.

WOODROW UNITED METHODIST CHURCH

1075 Woodrow Road, Woodrow

The Woodrow Methodist Church is considered the "mother" of all of Staten Island's Methodist churches. The first burials in its cemetery took place in 1787. Here is a postcard of Woodrow Methodist Church and Cemetery, circa 1907. *Gift of William T. Davis, Staten Island Museum.*

This congregation began in 1771 when Bishop Francis Asbury, founder of Methodism in America, came from New Jersey to preach at the home of Peter Van Pelt, a farmer. The first building on the site was constructed in 1787, when interments at the burial ground also began. This white clapboard church, dedicated in 1842, is surrounded by an eighteenth-century cemetery, making it a rare survivor of rural Staten Island. The portico of four large Doric columns and plain architrave with finely proportioned gable is strikingly beautiful in its simplicity. The ornate square bell tower in the Italianate style was added in 1876. Originally called the Woodrow Methodist Episcopal Church, this church is considered to be the "mother" of all Staten Island's Methodist churches. The Greek Revival structure became a designated New York City landmark in 1967.

ROSSVILLE AFRICAN METHODIST EPISCOPAL (AME) ZION CHURCH AND CEMETERY

SEE ARCHITECTURE

MAGYAR (HUNGARIAN) REFORMED CHURCH

19 Winant Place, Charleston

This New York City landmark was built in 1883 as St. Peter's German Evangelical Church by German industrialist and immigrant Balthazar

Kreischer. Like nearby housing and schools, it was meant to benefit brick workers at his factory built in 1855. Today's congregation still uses the original German-built pipe organ. Formerly called Kreischerville, the area's name was changed to Charleston during World War I. By then, a wave of Hungarian migration had already begun to transform the community. The Hungarians began practicing their Protestant faith here, and in 1919, they purchased the church complex that remains the center of their religious, cultural and social activities.

SAINT JOACHIM AND SAINT ANNE'S CHURCH

6581 Hylan Boulevard, Pleasant Plains

SEE ALSO EDUCATION AND HEALTH, ENVIRONMENT AND SPORTS

On September 8, 1887, Father John Drumgoole broke ground for Saint Joachim and Saint Anne's Church at the Mission for the Immaculate Virgin for the Protection of Homeless and Destitute Children. When completed in 1891, it was the largest church on Staten Island. After a 1973 fire destroyed most of the structure, leaving only the steeple and four walls standing, the church was rebuilt in 1976. The site is better known as Mount Loretto.

Completed in 1891, Saint Joachim and Saint Anne Church of Mount Loretto was the largest church on Staten Island. Here is a postcard, circa 1910, by William J. Grimshaw. *Gift of William T. Davis, Staten Island Museum.*

WARD'S POINT ARCHAEOLOGICAL SITE

Conference House Park, Tottenville

SEE ALSO ETHNICITY AND IMMIGRATION

Since 1858, remains and artifacts of Staten Island's original pre-European indigenous population have been found at this site. Flint chips, projectile points, pottery shards, net sinkers, fire-cracked stones and shells left behind by these former residents have been discovered. In 1982, the New York State Office of Parks, Recreation and Historic Preservation announced that the Ward's Point Conservation Area would be listed on the State and National Register of Historic Places. The burial ground serves as an important archaeological site and allows for important studies of early human settlements.

BEDELL-PIZZO FUNERAL HOME

7447 Amboy Road, Tottenville

Founded by Isaac Prey Bedell in 1841, what is now the Bedell-Pizzo Funeral Home is the oldest funeral home in New York City. Isaac was a carpenter who made cabinets when he transitioned into the more lucrative coffin-making business. In 1991, the 150th anniversary of the business was celebrated with the establishment of the Bedell Funeral Home Museum. Photos, embalming equipment, a makeup case, candelabras, coffins, crucifixes and funeral bills were put on display alongside the original beaver scarf and top hat that Isaac wore while working.

STATEN ISLAND BUDDHIST VIHARA

115 John Street, Port Richmond

Once required to travel to the New York Buddhist Vihara in Queens, local Sri Lankans and other Buddhists' dreams were realized in 1999 with the construction of this vihara. Devotees pay homage to the Triple Gem, the giant gold-toned Buddha (teacher), the Dhamma (teachings) and the

Sangha (monks). Twice a month, Dhamma school classes are held. In May, the Vesek, a holy day celebrating Buddha's birth, enlightenment and death, is celebrated by hundreds dressed in white. The Staten Island Sri Lankan community was very active in raising funds after the December 2004 tsunami, including working to rebuild Matara, a Sri Lankan village. Visitors are welcome to enter the garden, maintained by resident monks.

REFORMED CHURCH OF STATEN ISLAND

54 Port Richmond Avenue, Port Richmond

A license to build a Dutch Reformed church was received in 1715, even though records for this location date to 1696. The first church was erected in 1716 but was destroyed by the British during the American Revolution because of the Patriot leanings of many of its congregants. On the church's façade is a plaque that honors members of the Mersereau family for their service to the Patriot cause. Some of the Mersereaus were involved in a spy ring that provided

One of the earliest churches on Staten Island, the original building for the Reformed Church of Staten Island at Port Richmond dates to 1716. The current structure was built in 1844–1845. *Courtesy of Staten Island Museum.*

General George Washington with vital information about the British military in the New York/New Jersey area. The church that now stands was built in 1844–1845. Because a graveyard existed in this area prior to the church, it was dubbed the Burial Place. The Reformed Church, the Sunday school and the cemetery are listed in the National Register of Historic Places and are New York City landmarks.

ST. PHILIP'S BAPTIST CHURCH

77 Bennett Street, Port Richmond

In 1877, John Taylor and Leroy Dungey of Virginia and James Poole of Staten Island organized a Baptist mission that met in Park Baptist Church, Port Richmond. Despite the prejudices of neighbors, in 1881, lawyer Alfred de Groot helped Thomas Dungey secure property for the North Shore Colored Baptist Mission at 134 Faber Street, dedicated Easter 1889. The pastor from 1954 to 1992, the Reverend Dr. William A. Epps Jr., oversaw the growth and relocation of the church to where it stands today, formerly home of Zion Lutheran Church. Epps became a civil rights activist, was jailed with Dr. Martin Luther King Jr. in Birmingham, Alabama, and served as a Protestant chaplain at Arthur Kill Correctional Facility.

TRINITY/FOUNTAIN/STATEN ISLAND CEMETERIES

Richmond Terrace at Alaska Street, West Brighton

In 1802, Trinity Cemetery opened on the site of a Native American burial ground. In 1829, a homestead graveyard was started by the family of Joseph Ryers. Henry Fountain possessed adjacent land that eventually held grave sites. Both are examples of nonsegregated nineteenth-century burial grounds. In 1840, these cemeteries merged to form Staten Island Cemetery. Veterans from the War of 1812 and the Civil War are buried here. The area is maintained by the Friends of Abandoned Cemeteries of Staten Island.

TEMPLE EMANU-EL

984 Post Avenue, Port Richmond

SEE ALSO ARCHITECTURE

Established in 1907, Temple Emanu-El had its foundation in the business community of Port Richmond. The Classical Revival building was designed to resemble the Great Synagogue of Warsaw. Built in 1928, the Educational Building provides space for educational programming and social gatherings.

Built in 1928, Temple Emanu-El was designed to resemble the Great Synagogue of Warsaw, Poland. *Courtesy of Staten Island Museum.*

Temple Emanu-El hosts Hebrew classes, the Jewish War Veterans, a Boy Scout troop and the Staten Island Jewish Historical Society. In 2007, Temple Emanu-El was placed on the National Register of Historic Places.

Second Asbury African Methodist Episcopal Church and Cemetery or Cherry Lane Cemetery

Forest Avenue and Livermore Avenue, Port Richmond (Built Over)

The Second Asbury African Methodist Episcopal Church was established after 1850. When the church closed around 1903, none of the deceased was relocated from the cemetery. The burial ground was also referred to as the Old Slaves Burying Ground or the Cherry Lane Cemetery. It is the final resting place for hundreds of African Americans, many of whom were former slaves. It was one of the few North Shore cemeteries where African Americans could be buried.

Holy Trinity/St. Nicholas Greek Orthodox Church

1641 Richmond Avenue, Bull's Head

In 1927, a group of twenty Greek immigrant families, many from the islands of Kos, Lemnos and Crete, founded the Greek Educational Society

"A COMMON PURPOSE, A HIGHER PURPOSE"

Rabbi Gerald Sussman, Temple Emanu-El and President of the Board, Project Hospitality

Sometimes, when it's very quiet and the sun streams through the 103-year-old windows of Temple Emanu-El, I like to ponder. I think about all of the prayers said in the sanctuary, which reflected extremes of joy and grief and every emotion in between. I think of all of the celebrations held within those walls, marking the turning points of life and of the great events in the history of our nation.

The same can be said for all of the houses of worship on Staten Island. They are places where the deepest moments of our personal lives, as well as the lives of our community and nation, are reflected. They are places where hopes are rekindled, spirits nurtured and strength gathered. They speak to the highest within each of us, the part of us that seeks to transcend the petty and everyday and reach toward G-d and the dream of a world based on justice and love.

Houses of worship were the first public buildings built on Staten Island. The Protestant churches of colonial times have been augmented, since the mid-nineteenth century, by Catholic churches, later by synagogues and, in more recent years, by mosques and Hindu and Buddhist temples.

The first Jewish immigrants came to Staten Island in the 1840s. By the 1890s, they organized the first synagogues in Tompkinsville (Congregation B'nai Jeshurun), Stapleton and Port Richmond. The building of the Verrazano bridge led to a further increase in the island's Jewish population. Today, most of the Jewish immigrants are from the former Soviet Union and Israel.

Though differing in doctrine, many congregations of diverse faiths are united in vision, in seeking a peaceful and humane community. They are working toward mutual understanding through efforts like the Building Bridges Coalition, Staten Island Clergy Leadership and Community Days.

For 350 years, faith has flourished on this island and continues to do so. The varieties of religious expression have grown; so has the ability of the various groups to come together for common purposes. The congregations of Staten Island, some housed in historic structures, others in storefronts and even private residences, continue to play their crucial role.

Aristotle, Inc. The Greek Orthodox church they started was composed mostly of immigrant farmers from Bull's Head, Travis and New Springville and store owners from Port Richmond. The Holy Trinity Greek Orthodox Church opened in 1930, while a larger church on Victory Boulevard opened in 1970. The annual Greek festival in September is one of Staten Island's most popular events.

SISTERS OF THE DISCIPLES OF THE DIVINE MASTER CHURCH

60 Sunset Avenue, Emerson Hill

Present today in twenty-eight countries, the Pious Disciples of the Divine Master were founded in Alba, Italy, in 1928 by James Alberione and in the United States in 1948. The Staten Island site is their U.S. headquarters. A women's congregation, they take care of elderly and infirm priests, produce stained-glass windows and express their faith in all art forms, including embroidery and statues.

HINDU TEMPLE OF STATEN ISLAND

1318 Victory Boulevard, Sunnyside

In the 1990s, the small Hindu community met monthly in local homes for prayer meetings or traveled to Flushing, Queens, or New Jersey. Desiring a dedicated space on Staten Island, the community purchased the property in 2001 and completed its building in 2007. The first deities were installed with chants, prayers and sacred baths of milk, yogurt and sugar. More than four hundred families pay homage here, amid the scent of sandlewood, to Sri Ganesha, who represents moving through obstacles; Sri Durga, who preserves moral order; and other deities. A Balavihir, school for young children, is also offered. In Dongan Hills, another one hundred families practice Hindu Mandir at Prem Prakash Temple (180 Burgher Avenue).

Silver Lake Cemetery

926 Victory Boulevard, Silver Lake

Silver Lake Cemetery is owned and operated by the Hebrew Free Burial Association (HFBA), which was founded in Manhattan in 1888. The burial ground was established in 1892 for low-income Jews who could not afford a proper burial. It is Staten Island's oldest Jewish cemetery. Silver Lake Cemetery accepted indigent burials until it reached its limit in 1909. Around this time, the HFBA purchased property at Richmond for the establishment of Mount Richmond Cemetery. The Hebrew Free Burial Association has provided sixty thousand burials on Staten Island.

B'nai Jeshurun

275 Martling Avenue, West New Brighton

The oldest Jewish congregation on Staten Island, B'nai Jeshurun was formed in 1884 when eleven families met in a rented Richmond Turnpike (now Victory Boulevard) space in Tompkinsville. The congregation moved to Martling Avenue in West Brighton in 1974. The following year, B'nai Jeshurun merged with Temple Tifereth Israel, a congregation that was organized in 1916. The Tifereth Israel building still stands on Wright Street in Stapleton and is now the First Central Baptist Church.

The Unitarian Church of Staten Island

312 Fillmore Street, New Brighton

The Unitarian church has its founding in the United Independent Christian Church at Stapleton and the Congregational Church at New Brighton. Both were incorporated in 1851. The following year they came together as the Church of the Redeemer. Opening in 1853, the first church stood on Victory Boulevard at Cebra Avenue. A reorganized church was established on December 2, 1868, at Clinton Avenue. Influential citizens, such as George W. Curtis, Minthorne Tompkins, Francis L. Hagadorn and Sidney Howard Gay, were involved with the church, which has maintained its civic activism to the present date.

THE STATEN ISLAND LEGACY TRAIL

Twenty-Five Sites to Discover

T ake a driving, biking or hiking tour to explore "One Island, Many Stories." For more information on sites, see relevant chapters.

1. **Bobby Thompson**, near Richmond County Savings Bank Ballpark, St. George.
2. **Langston Hughes**, near Staten Island Ferry, St. George.
3. **Staten Island Borough Hall**, 10 Richmond Terrace, St. George.
4. **African American Loyalists/Watering Place**, intersection of Victory Boulevard and Bay Street, Tompkinsville.
5. **Breweries/immigrant entrepreneurs**, Tappen Park, 105 Water Street.
6. **Our Lady of Mount Carmel**, 36 Amity Street, Rosebank.
7. **NYC Marathon**, starting point, New York Avenue and Battery Road.
8. **FDR Boardwalk and Hoffman and Swinburne Islands**, Father Capodanno Boulevard, South Beach.
9. **Staten Island University Hospital**, 475 Seaview Avenue, Midland Beach.
10. **Miller Field**, 440 New Dorp Lane, New Dorp.
11. **Historic Richmond Town's Voorlezer's House**, 62 Arthur Kill Road, Richmond.
12. **St. Andrew's Church and Cemetery**, 40 Old Mill Road, Richmond.

13. **Staten Island Airport** (Former Site), 2655 Richmond Avenue, Staten Island Mall, New Springville.
14. **Frederick Law Olmsted House**, 4515 Hylan Boulevard, Eltingville.
15. **Paul Zindel**, 1000 Luten Avenue, Tottenville High School.
16. **Kreischerville Worker Housing**, 71 Kreischer Street.
17. **Supreme Chocolatier**, 1150 South Avenue, Bloomfield.
18. **High Rock Park, Ohrbach Lake and Greenbelt Nature Center**, 700 Rockland Avenue, Egbertville.
19. **Bayonne Bridge**, near Port Richmond High School, Port Richmond.
20. **"Commodore" Cornelius Vanderbilt Birthplace**, 2175 Richmond Terrace, Faber Park, Port Richmond.
21. **Native American History**, Alaska Street and Richmond Terrace, New Brighton.
22. **Abolitionists/women's suffrage**, Curtis, Shaw and Gay Homes, 400 Henderson Avenue, Livingston.
23. **Chinese Scholar's Garden**, Snug Harbor Cultural Center, 1000 Richmond Terrace.
24. **Little Sri Lanka**, 322 Victory Boulevard, Tompkinsville.
25. **St. Paul's Avenue Historic District**, 309 St. Paul's Avenue, Stapleton.

Staten Island
Legacy Trail

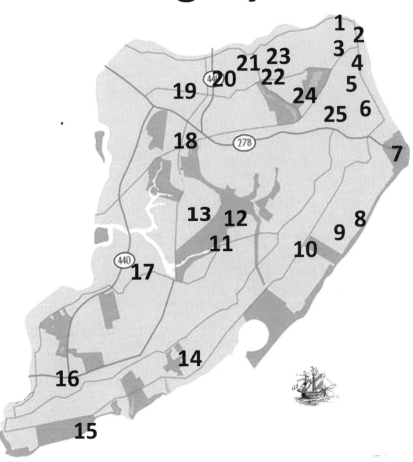

LIST OF STATEN ISLAND BOROUGH PRESIDENTS

George Cromwell (Republican, 1898–1913)
Charles J. McCormack (Democrat, 1914–1915)
Calvin D. Van Name (Democrat, 1915–1921)
Mathew Cahill (Democrat, 1922)
John A. Lynch (Democrat, 1922–1933)
Joseph A. Palma (Republican, 1934–1945)
Cornelius A. Hall (Democrat, 1946–1953)
Edward Baker (Democrat, 1953–1954)
Albert V. Maniscalco (Democrat, 1954–1965)
Robert T. Connor (Republican, Conservative, Democrat, 1966–1977)
Anthony Gaeta (Republican, 1977–1984)
Ralph Lamberti (Democrat, 1984–1989)
Guy V. Molinari (Republican, 1990–2001)
James Molinaro (Conservative, 2002–present)

SI350 BOARD MEMBERS AND COMMITTEES

SI350 BOARD OF DIRECTORS

Robert Coghlan (President and Chairman of the Board)
BNP Paribas, managing director/chief regulatory officer

Steven Decker (Secretary)
Decker, Decker, Dito & Internicola, partner

Linda Baran
Staten Island Chamber of Commerce, president and CEO

Al Curtis
Global Capital Ltd., executive vice-president

Aurelia Curtis
Curtis High School, principal

Dr. Richard Guarasci
Wagner College, president

Gerard McEnerney
St. John's University, AVP and executive director

Dr. Ann Merlino
Retired educator, College of Staten Island, professor emeritus

Dr. Tomas Morales
College of Staten Island, president

Leticia Remauro
Community Board 1, chair

Henry Salmon
Equity Valuation Associates, CEO

SI350 ADVISORY BOARD

Tom Matteo: chair and Staten Island Borough historian
Jack Eichenbaum: Queens Borough historian
Michael Miscione: Manhattan Borough historian
Ron Schweiger: Brooklyn Borough historian
Lloyd Ultan: Bronx Borough historian

SI350 HISTORIANS AND EDUCATORS

Lori R. Weintrob, chair; Rosette Allegretti, Larry Anderson, Felicity Beil, Margaret Bérci, Mary Elizabeth Brown, Mary L. Bullock, Lee Covino, Christopher Cuccia, Sylvia D'Alessandro, Carlotta DeFillo, Cara Dellatte, Linda Eskenas, Nicole Fenton, Joe Ferlazzo, Susan Fowler, Cathie Gelman, Kenneth M. Gold, Chan Graham, Carin Guarasci, Margaret Haley, Linda Hauck, Rachel Jirka, Tina Kaasmann-Dunn, James Kaser, Jessica Kratz, Josephina Lee, Ruth Lasser, Peter Levine, Mirjana Luczun, Charles Markis, Joseph Margiotta, Ciro Matrecano, Thomas Matteo, Diane Matyas, Bonnie McCourt, Gerard McEnerney, Ron Meisels, Christopher Mulé, Dorothy Jensen Myhre-Donahue, Deborah Nasta, Jeannine Otis, Phillip Papas, Chuck Perry, Stephen Preskill, Jay Price, Lynn Rogers, J. Fred Rodriquez, Carl Rutberg, Arleen Ryback, Charles Sachs, Steve Salgo, Patricia Salmon, Barnett Shepherd, Amy Stempler, Kristin Teasdale, Patricia Tooker, Meg Ventrudo, Ronald Washington and Andrew Wilson.

SI350 ACADEMIC CONFERENCE/EDUCATION SYMPOSIUM COMMITTEE

Margaret Bérci and Phillip Papas, co-chairs; Rosette Allegretti, Winnie Brophy, Richard Flanagan, Blythe Hinitz, Christopher Mulé, Christopher Pennington, Patricia Salmon, Patricia Tooker, Lori R. Weintrob, Andrew Wilson and Adam Zalma.

SI350 TECHNOLOGY COMMITTEE

Johnny Chin (www.si350.org website administrator) and Andrew Wilson, co-chairs; Sarah Clark, Gregory Colletti, Anthony Lociano and Jason Wickersty.

SI350 PARENTS COMMITTEE

Josephina Lee and Cathie Gelman, co-chairs; Addy Manipella and Lorraine Danishewski.

SI350 PUBLIC RELATIONS COMMITTEE

LaTesha Bourne, Lee Manchester, David Picerno and Jason Wickersty.

BIBLIOGRAPHY

Baugher, Sherene. "Trade Networks: Colonial and Federal Period (1680–1815)." *Proceedings of the Staten Island Institute of Arts and Sciences* 34 (1989): 33–37.

Bayles, Richard M. *History of Richmond County, Staten Island, New York: From Its Discovery to the Present Time.* New York: L.E. Preston and Company, 1887.

Clute, John J. *Annals of Staten Island: From Its Discovery to the Present Time.* New York: Press of Charles Vogt, 1877.

Cudahy, Brian J. *Over and Back: The History of Ferryboats in New York Harbor.* New York: Fordham University Press, 1990.

Davis, William T. *The Conference/Billopp House.* Staten Island, NY: Staten Island Historical Society, 1926.

De Veaux, Alexis. *Warrior Poet: A Biography of Audre Lorde.* New York: W.W. Norton & Company, Inc., 2004.

Dickenson, Richard. *Holden's Staten Island: A History of Richmond County.* New York: Center for Migration Studies, 2002.

Duncan, Russell, ed. *Blue-Eyed Child of Fortune: The Civil War Letters of Colonel Robert Gould Shaw.* Athens: University of Georgia Press, 1992.

Foote, Lorien. *Seeking the One Great Remedy: Francis George Shaw and Nineteenth Century Reform.* Athens: Ohio University Press, 2003.

Hix, Charlotte M. *Staten Island Wills and Letters of Administration: Richmond County, 1670–1800.* Bowie, MD: Heritage Books, 1993.

Hughes, Langston. *The Big Sea.* New York, A.A. Knopf, 1940.

Katchen, Alan S. *Abel Kiviat, National Champion: Twentieth-Century Track & Field and the Melting Pot.* Syracuse, NY: Syracuse University Press, 2009.

Leng, Charles W., and William T. Davis. *Staten Island and Its People: A History, 1609–1929.* 3 vols. New York: Lewis Historical Publishing, 1930.

Matteo, Thomas W. *Staten Island: I Didn't Know That!* Virginia Beach, VA: Donning Company Publishers, 2009.

Morris, Ira K. *Morris's Memorial History of Staten Island, New York.* 2 vols. New York: Memorial Publishing, 1898–1900.

Mosley, Lois A. *Sandy Ground Memories.* Staten Island, NY: Staten Island Historical Society, 2003.

Papas, Phillip. *That Ever Loyal Island: Staten Island and the American Revolution.* New York: New York University Press, 2007.

Papas, Phillip, and Lori R. Weintrob. *Port Richmond.* Charleston, SC: Arcadia Publishing, 2009.

Price, Jay. *Thanksgiving, 1959: When One Corner of New York City Was Still Part of Small-Town America and High School Football Was the Last Thing Guys Did for Love.* Pennington, NJ: Mountain Lion Inc., 2009.

Rosenfeld, Michael, and Charles LaCerra, eds. *Community, Continuity, and Change: New Perspectives on Staten Island History.* New York: Pace University Press, 1999.

Sachs, Charles L. *Made on Staten Island: Agriculture, Industry, and Suburban Living in the City.* Staten Island, NY: Staten Island Historical Society, 1988.

———. "Staten Island." In *The Encyclopedia of New York City*, Second Edition, edited by Kenneth T. Jackson. New Haven, CT: Yale University Press, 2010.

Salmon, Patricia M. *Realms of History: The Cemeteries of Staten Island.* Staten Island, NY: Staten Island Museum, 2006.

———. *The Staten Island Ferry: A History.* Staten Island, NY: Staten Island Museum, 2009.

Shepherd, Barnett. *Tottenville, The Town the Oyster Built: A Staten Island Community Its People, Industry, and Architecture.* Staten Island, NY: Preservation League of Staten Island and the Tottenville Historical Society, 2008.

Stiles, T.J. *The Epic Life of Cornelius Vanderbilt.* New York: Random House, Inc., 2009.

Venables, Robert W. "A Historical Overview of Staten Island's Trade Networks." *Proceedings of the Staten Island Institute of Arts and Sciences* 34 (1989): 1–24.

Wilson, Andrew. "Langston Hughes: A Season on Staten Island." *Staten Island Historian* 21 (Winter 2010): 1–7.

INDEX

ABOUT THE CONTRIBUTORS

Kenneth M. Gold, associate professor of education, College of Staten Island/CUNY, is the author of *School's In: The History of Summer Education in American Public Schools* and is currently working on *The Forgotten Borough*, a history of Staten Island in the early twentieth century.

James A. Kaser, professor and archivist at the College of Staten Island/CUNY, earned a doctorate in American studies from Bowling Green State University and is the author of three books.

Jessica R. Kratz, Greenbelt Nature Center coordinator and a past Department of Environmental Conservation Camp scholarship recipient, has found a muse and a life path along woodland trails.

Christopher Mulé serves as director of folk life and deputy director for the Council on the Arts & Humanities on Staten Island (COAHSI). He holds a master's degree in folklore and ethnomusicology from Indiana University, Bloomington.

Phillip Papas is associate professor of history, Union County College, and author of *That Ever Loyal Island: Staten Island and the American Revolution* (2007) and *Port Richmond* with Lori R. Weintrob (2009).

Jay Price, a longtime columnist for the *Staten Island Advance*, is the author of *Thanksgiving 1959*, a chronicle of life and sports on Staten Island.

Charles L. Sachs is former senior curator of the New York Transit Museum and chief curator at the Staten Island Historical Society. He is author of *Made on Staten Island: Agriculture, Industry, and Suburban Living in the City* (1988) and numerous articles on the history and material culture of Staten Island and the metropolitan region.

Patricia M. Salmon is the curator of history at the Staten Island Museum. She is the author of *Realms of History: The Cemeteries of Staten Island* and *The Staten Island Ferry: A History*.

Barnett Shepherd, an independent architectural historian and local history author, was executive director of the Staten Island Historical Society from 1981 to 2000. His most recent book, *Tottenville: The Town the Oyster Built* (2009), won an Award of Merit from the American Association for State and Local History.

Patricia Tooker, assistant professor and director of Undergraduate Nursing Studies at Wagner College, received her BSN, MSN and FNP from Wagner College.

Meg Ventrudo, executive director of the Jacques Marchais Museum of Tibetan Art, received a master's of arts in history from George Mason University. She was born and raised on Staten Island.

Lori Weintrob, chair and associate professor of history at Wagner College, is co-chair of si350, Inc., and coauthor (with Phillip Papas) of *Port Richmond* (2009).

Andrew Wilson has been a librarian at the New York Public Library for over twenty years in Staten Island and Manhattan. He has a bachelor's of arts in history from Lafayette College and a master's degree in library science from the University of South Florida.